ROCKET PUBLISHING

PUBLISHED IN 2018 BY
ROCKET PUBLISHING

PRINTED IN THE UNITED STATE OF AMERICA

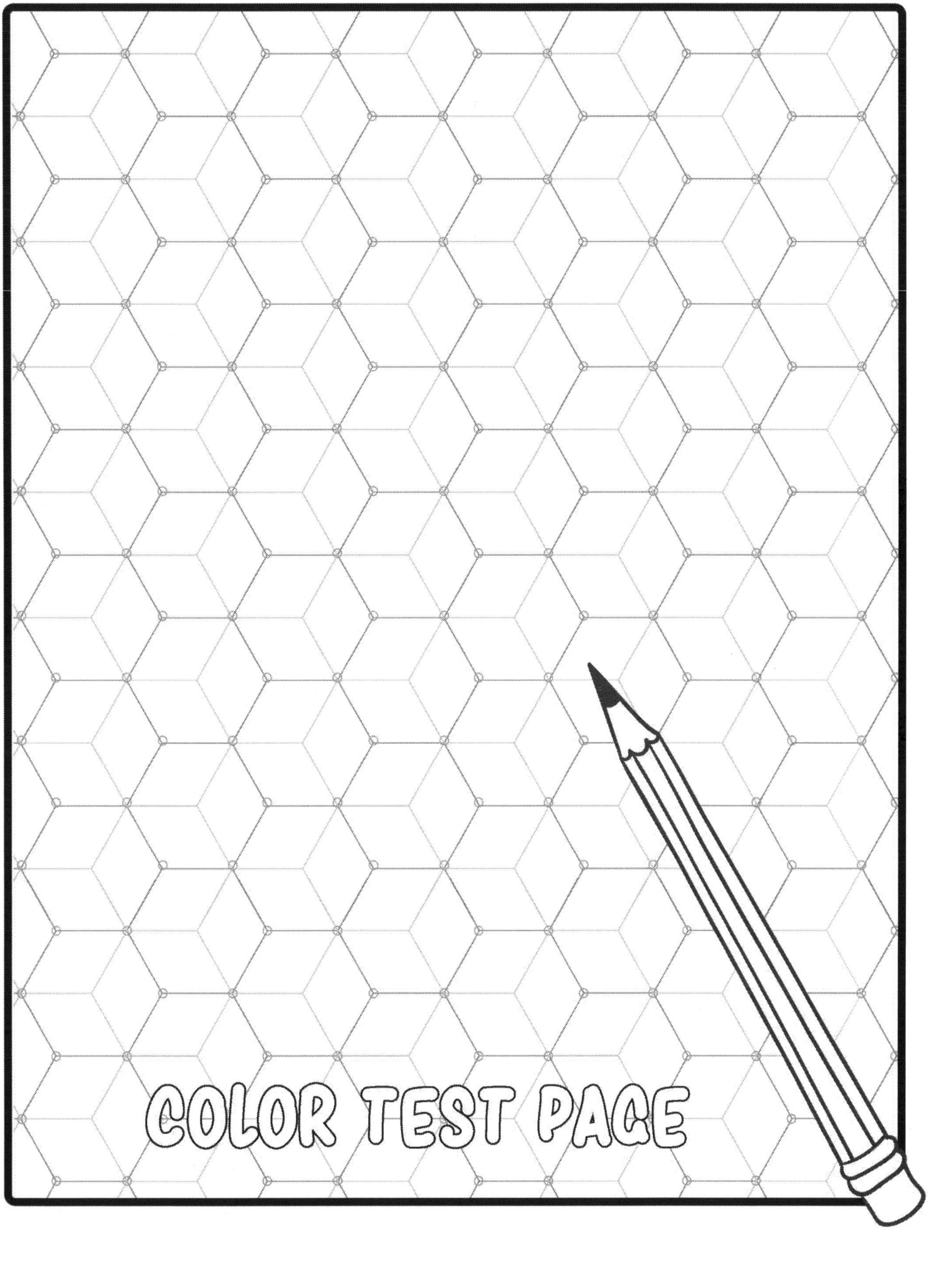
COLOR TEST PAGE

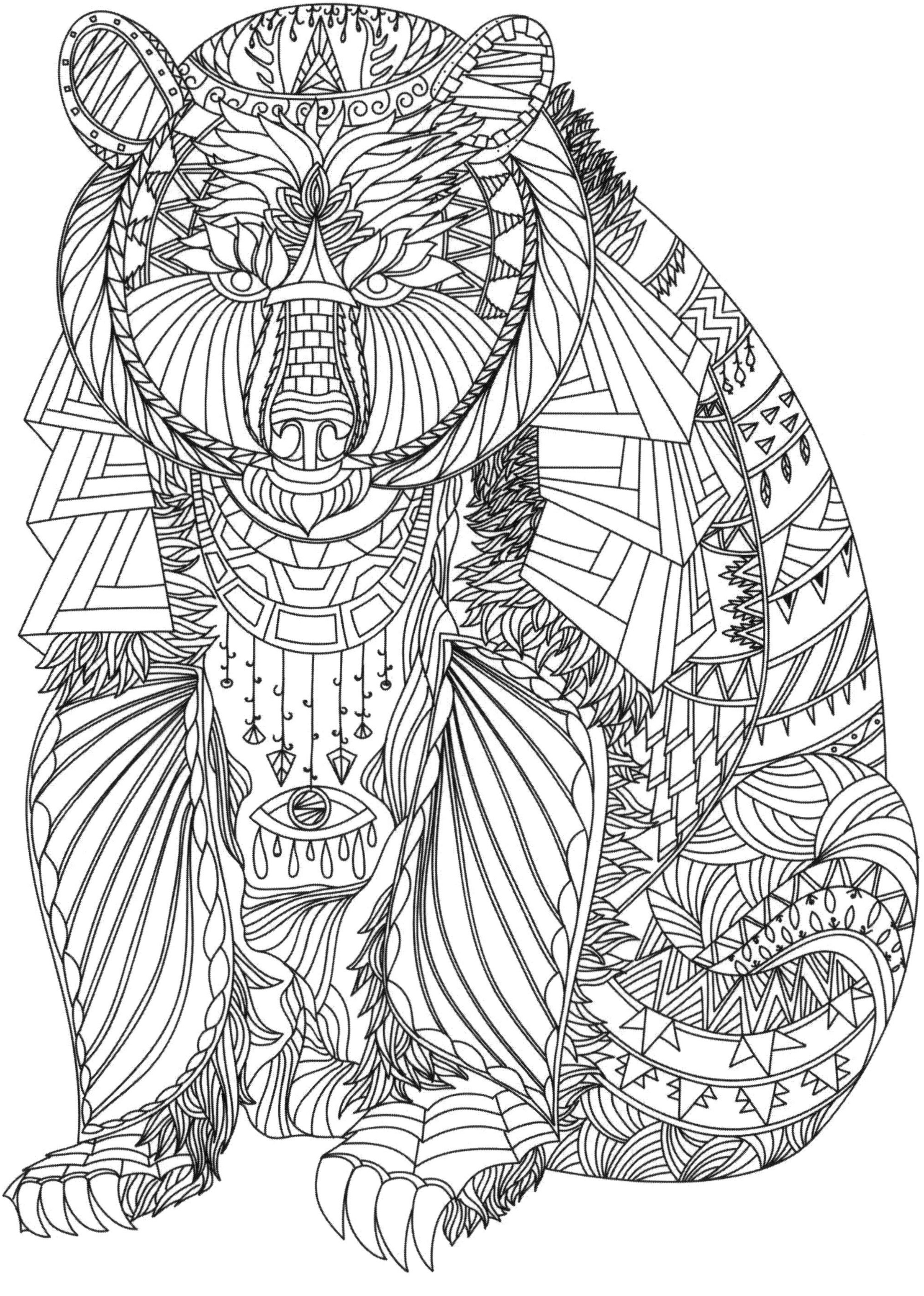

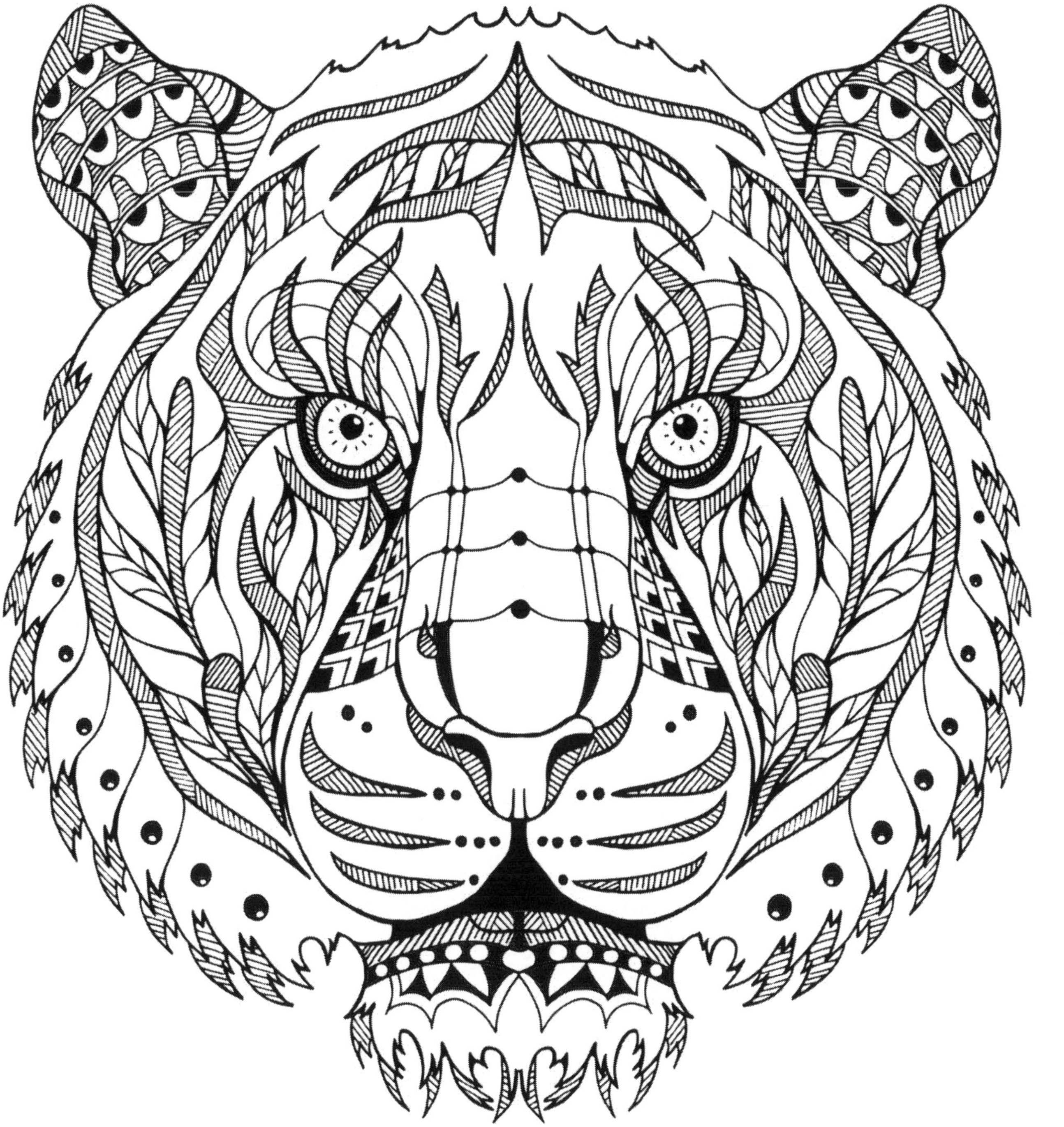

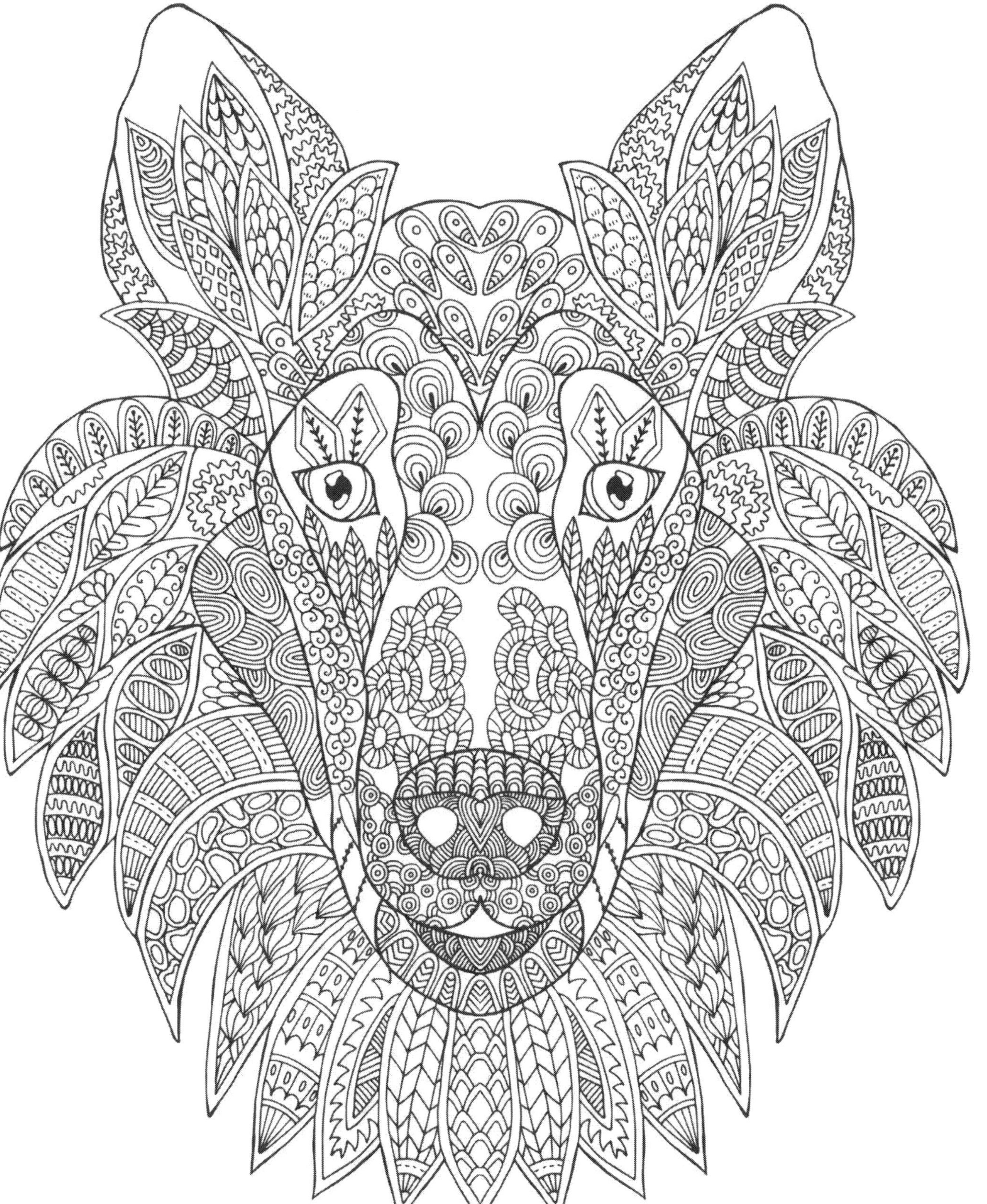

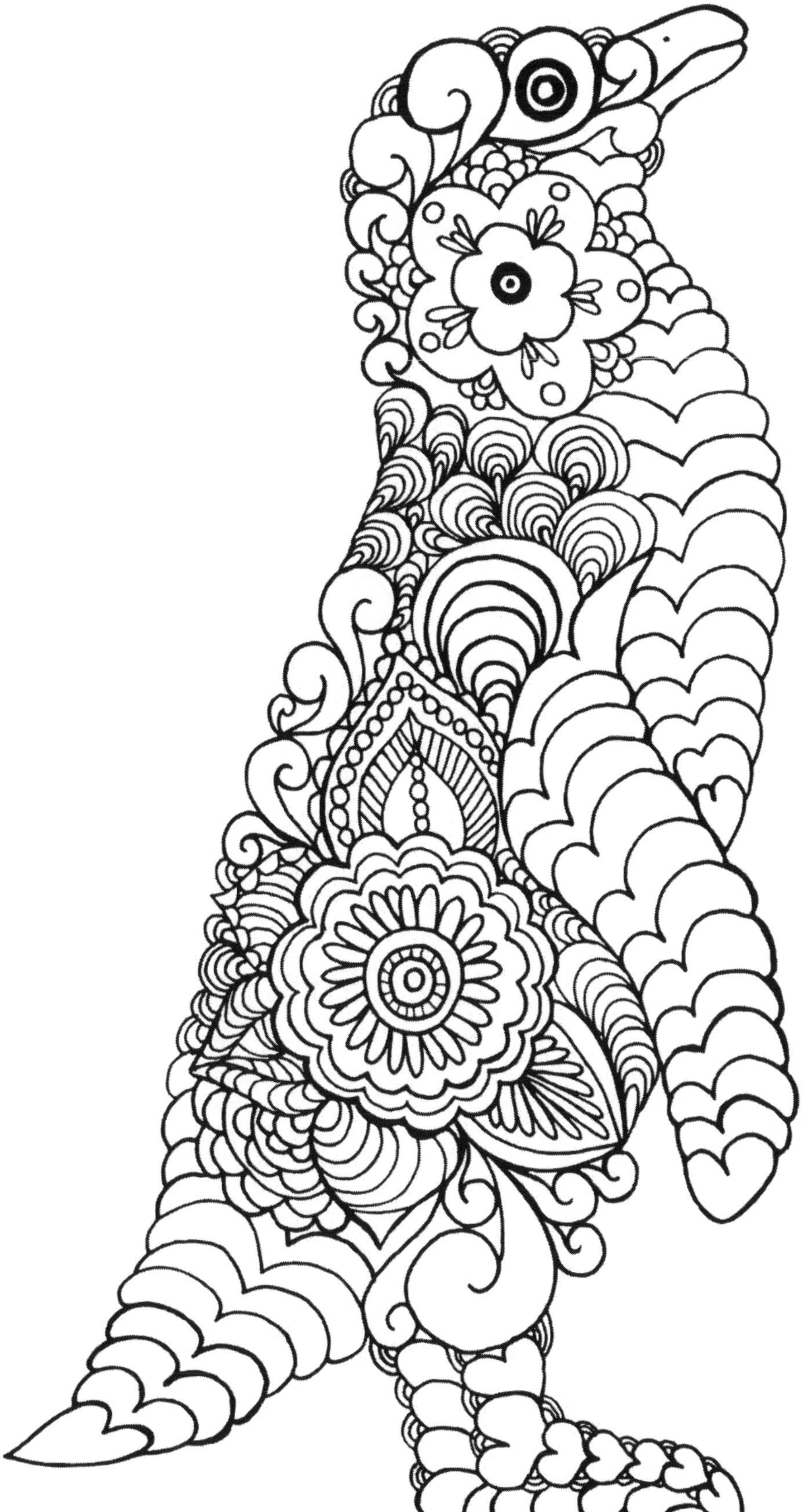

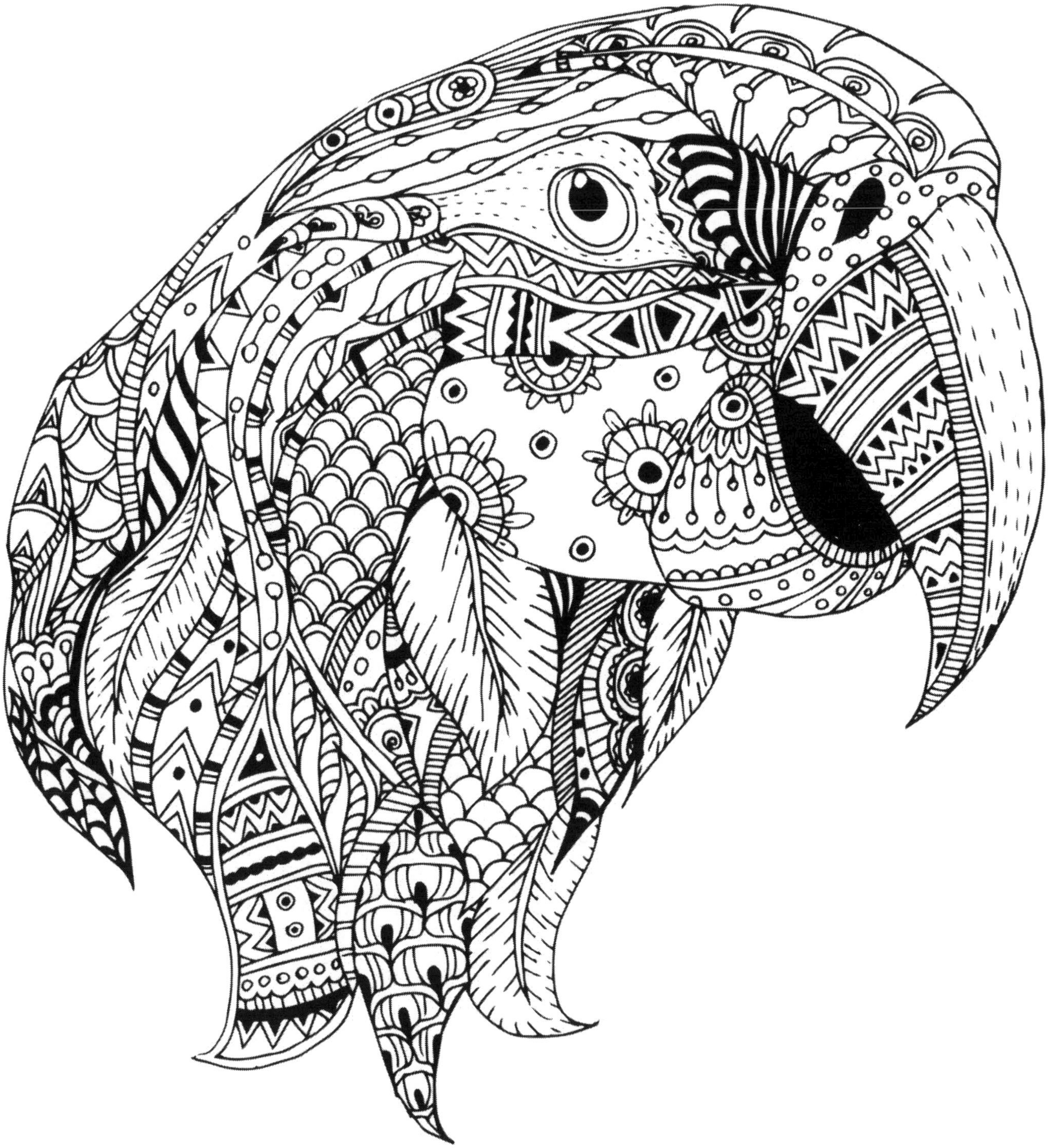

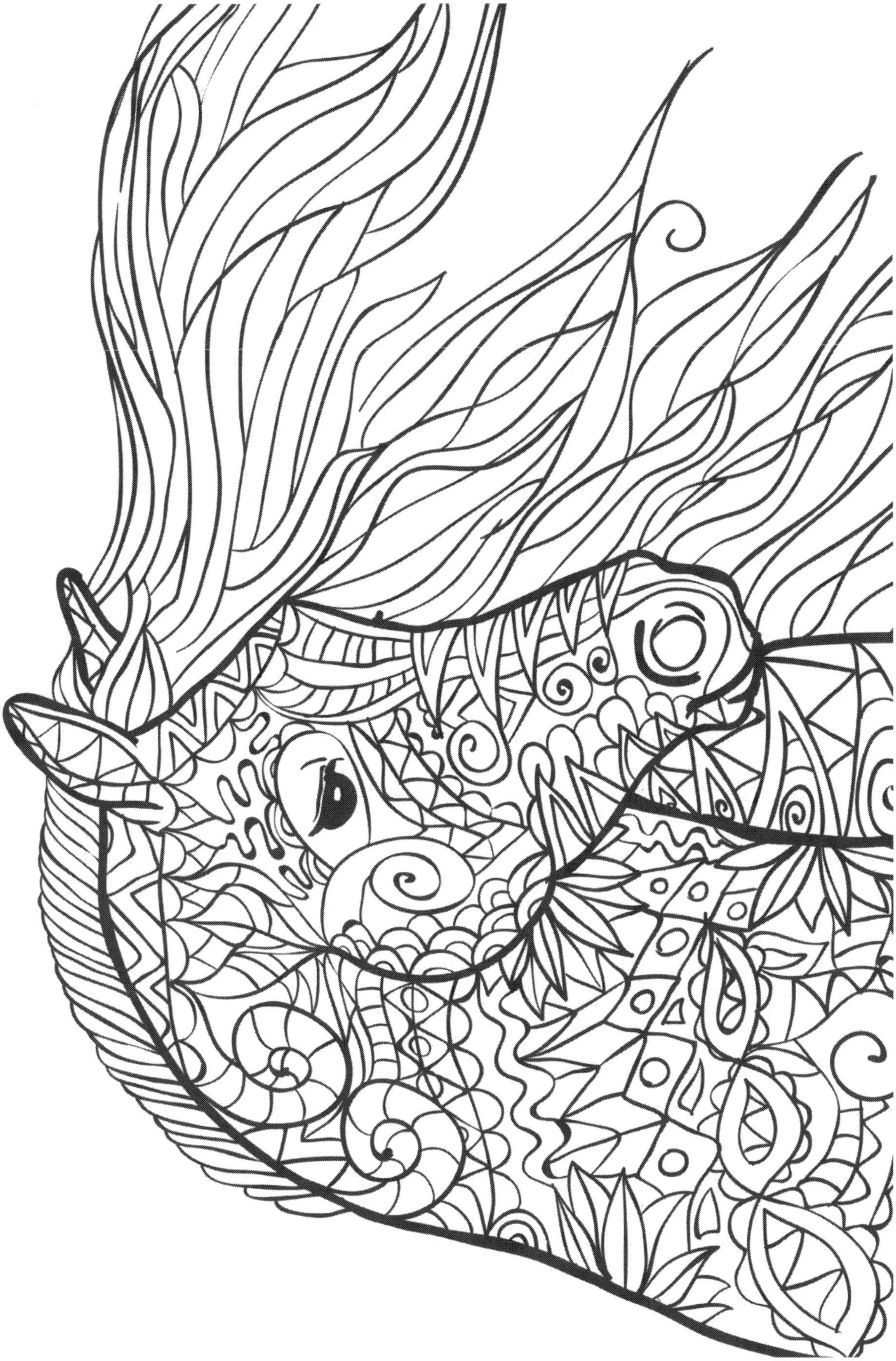

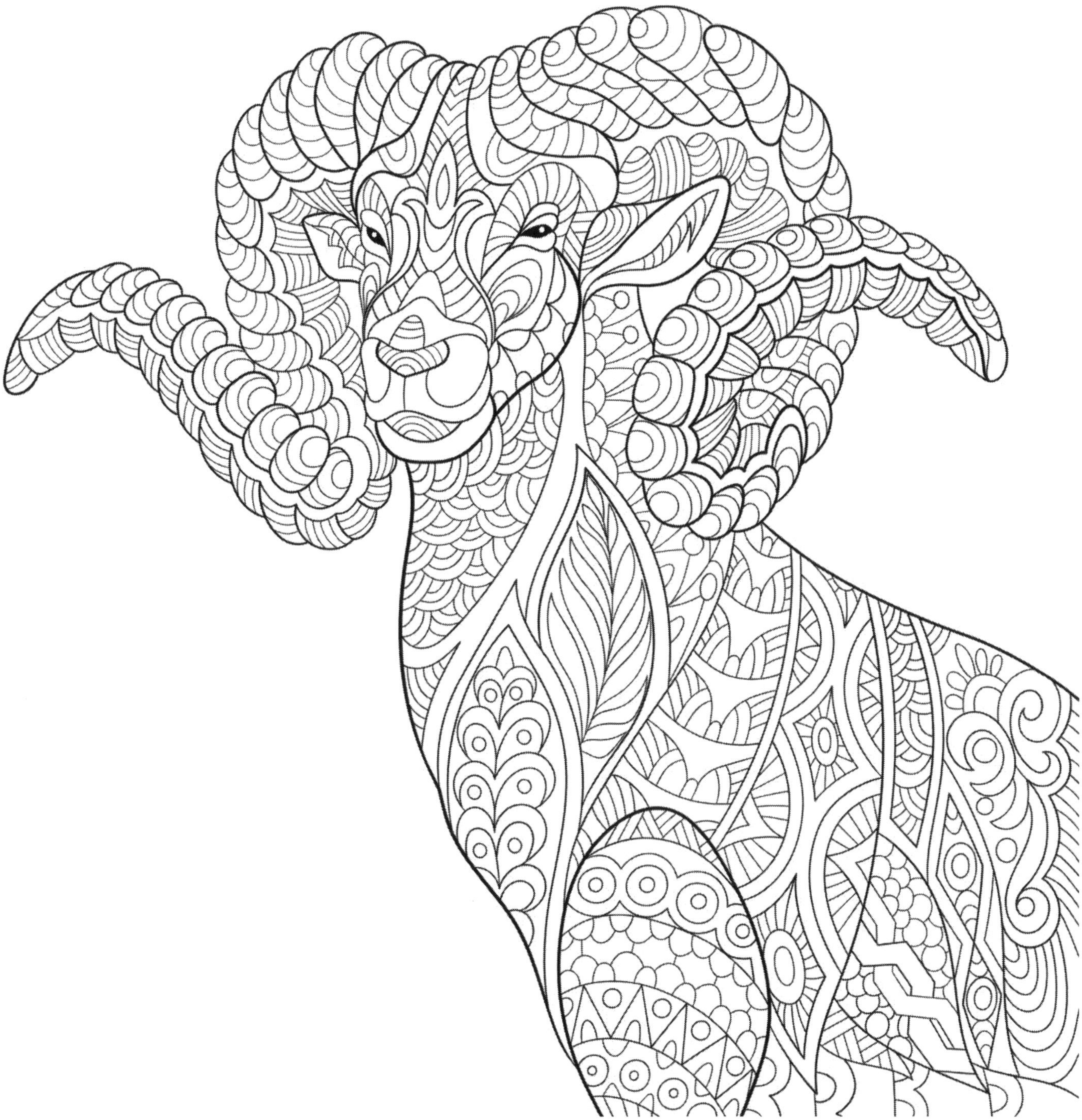

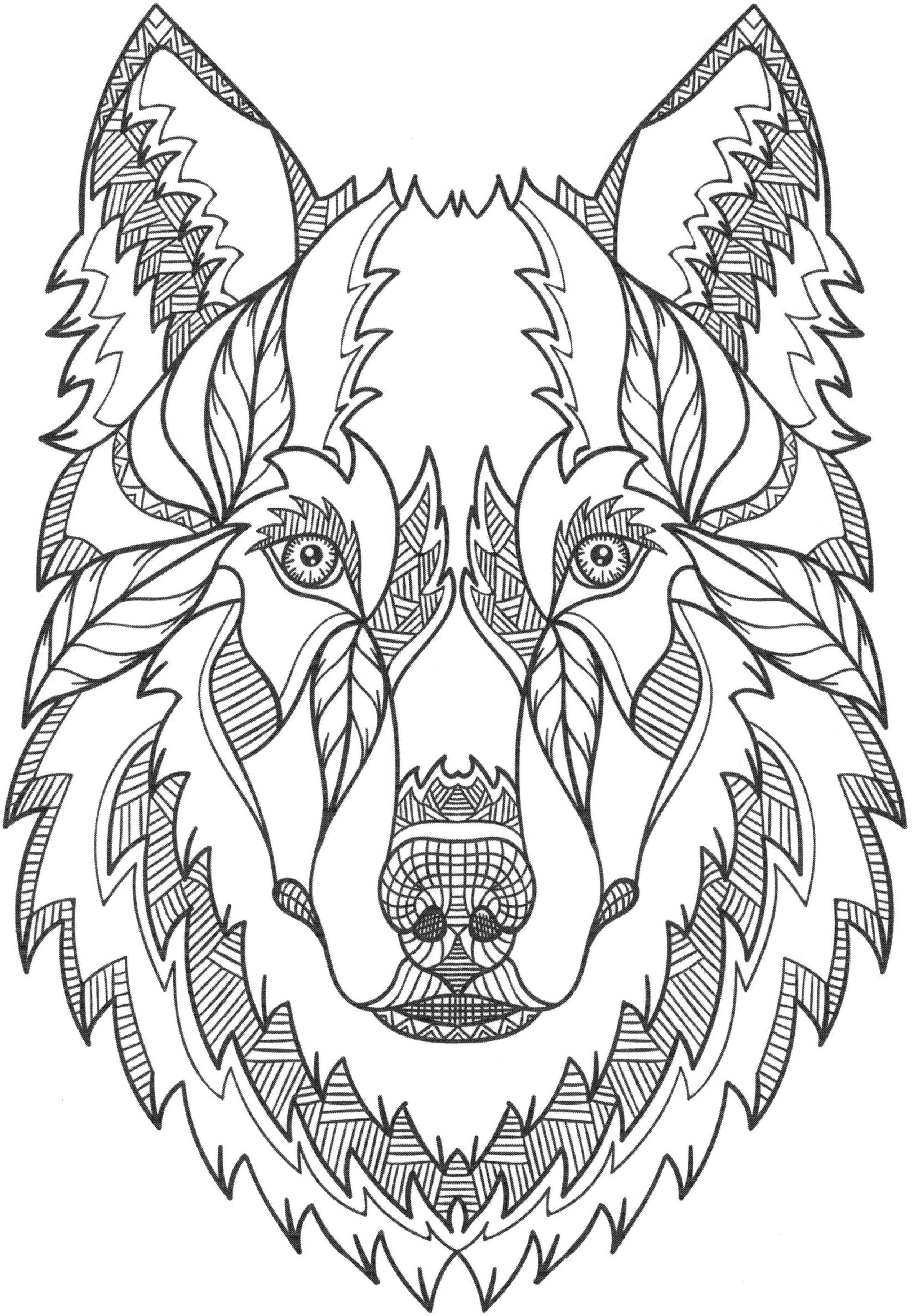

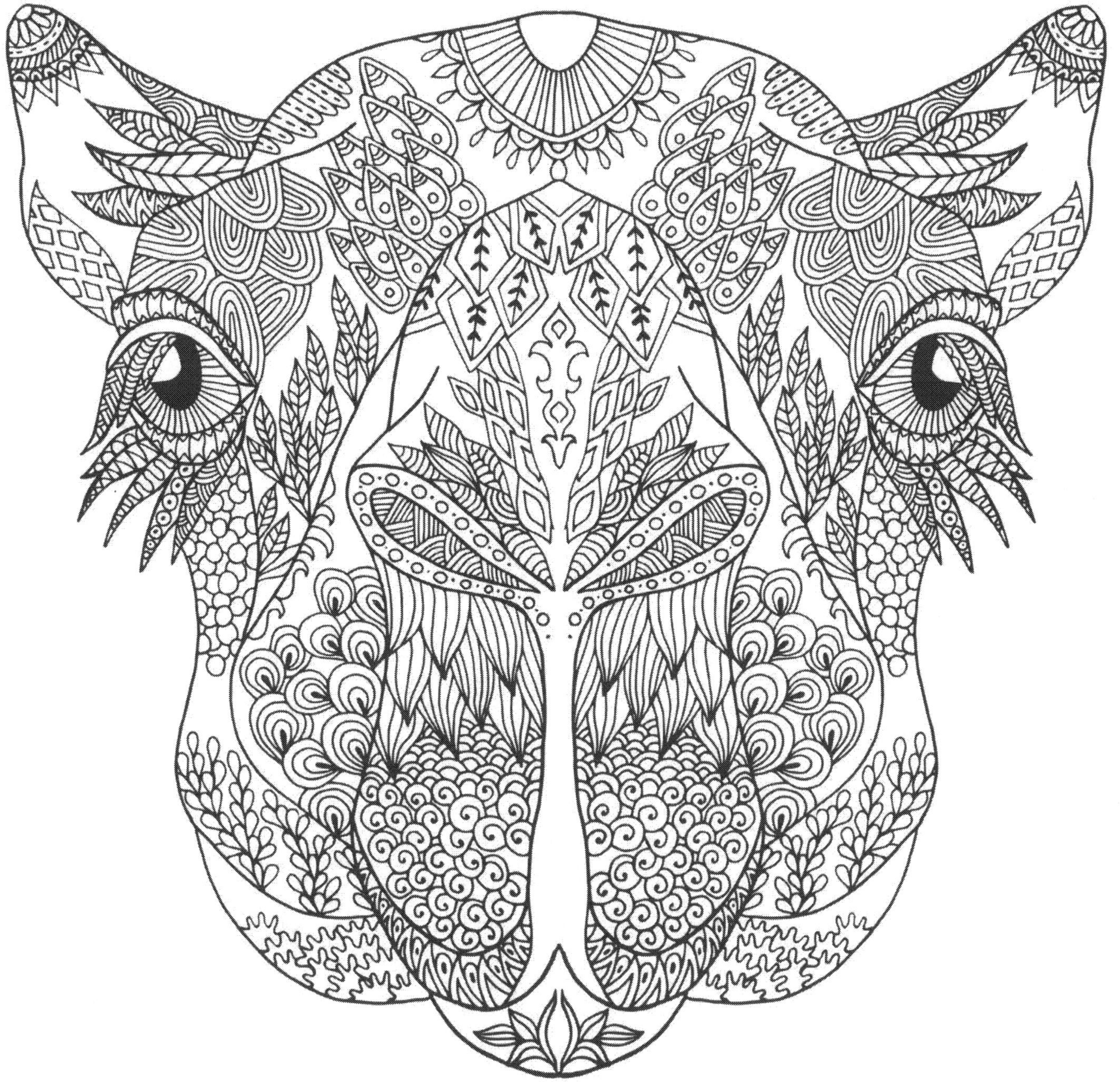

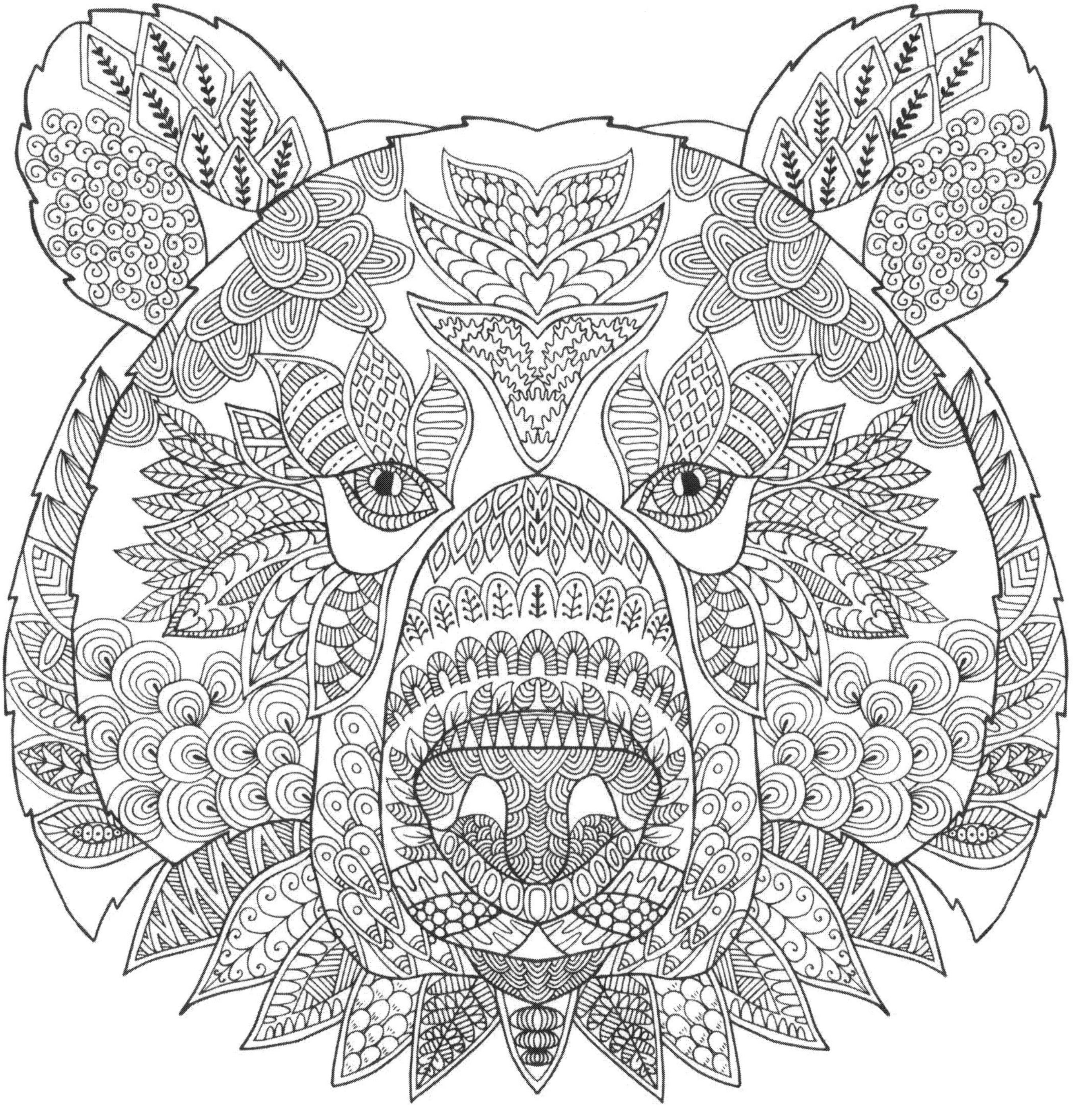

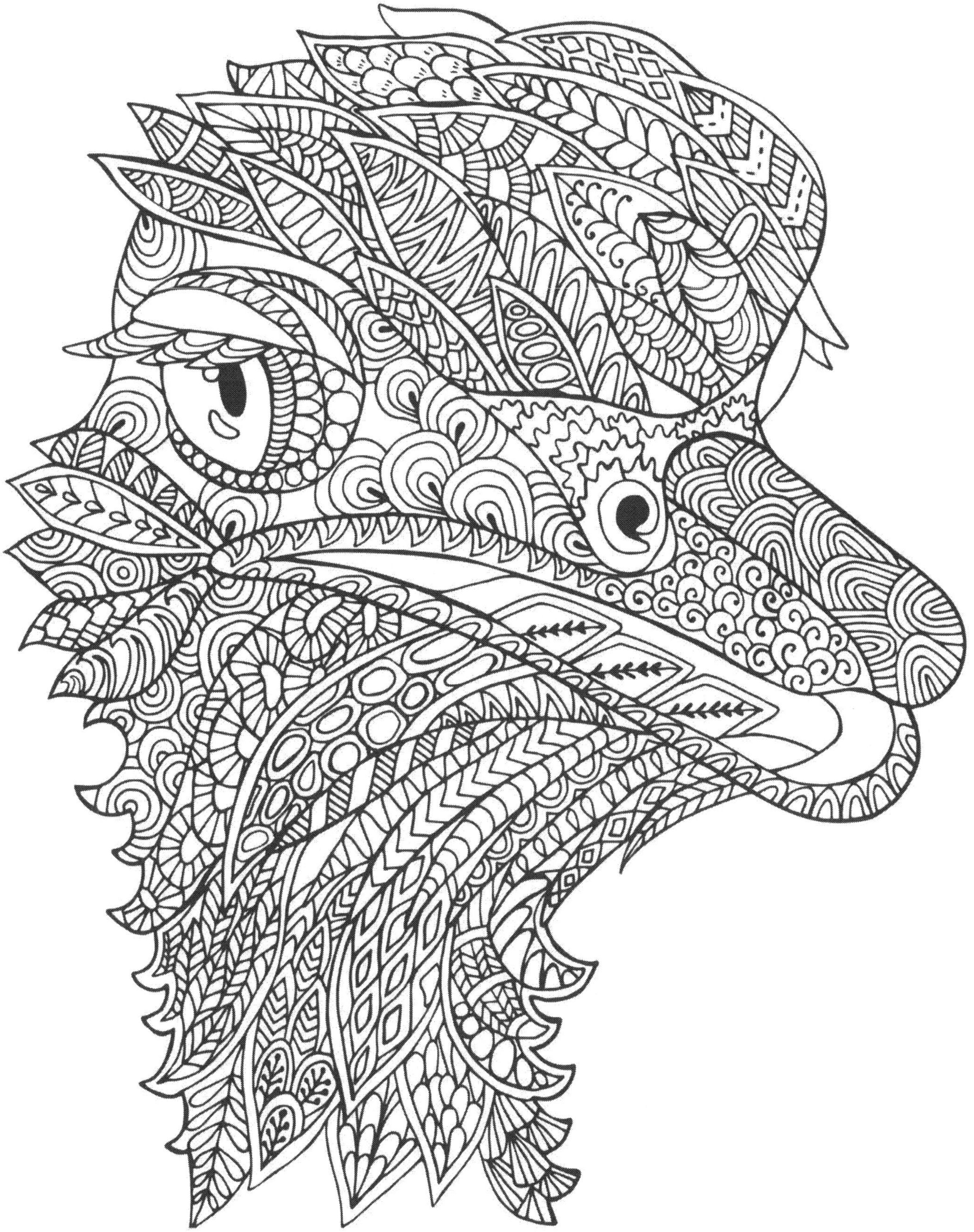

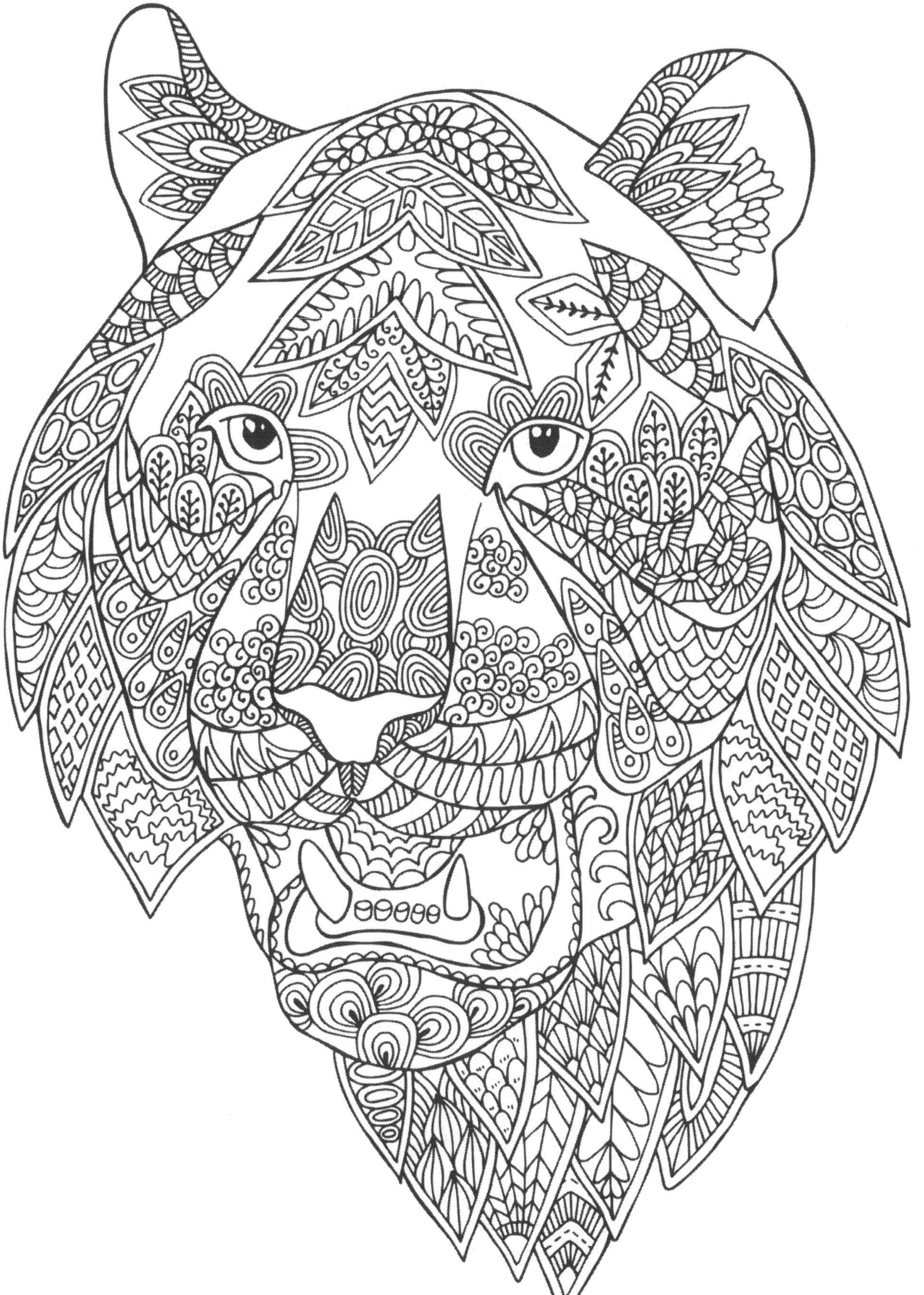

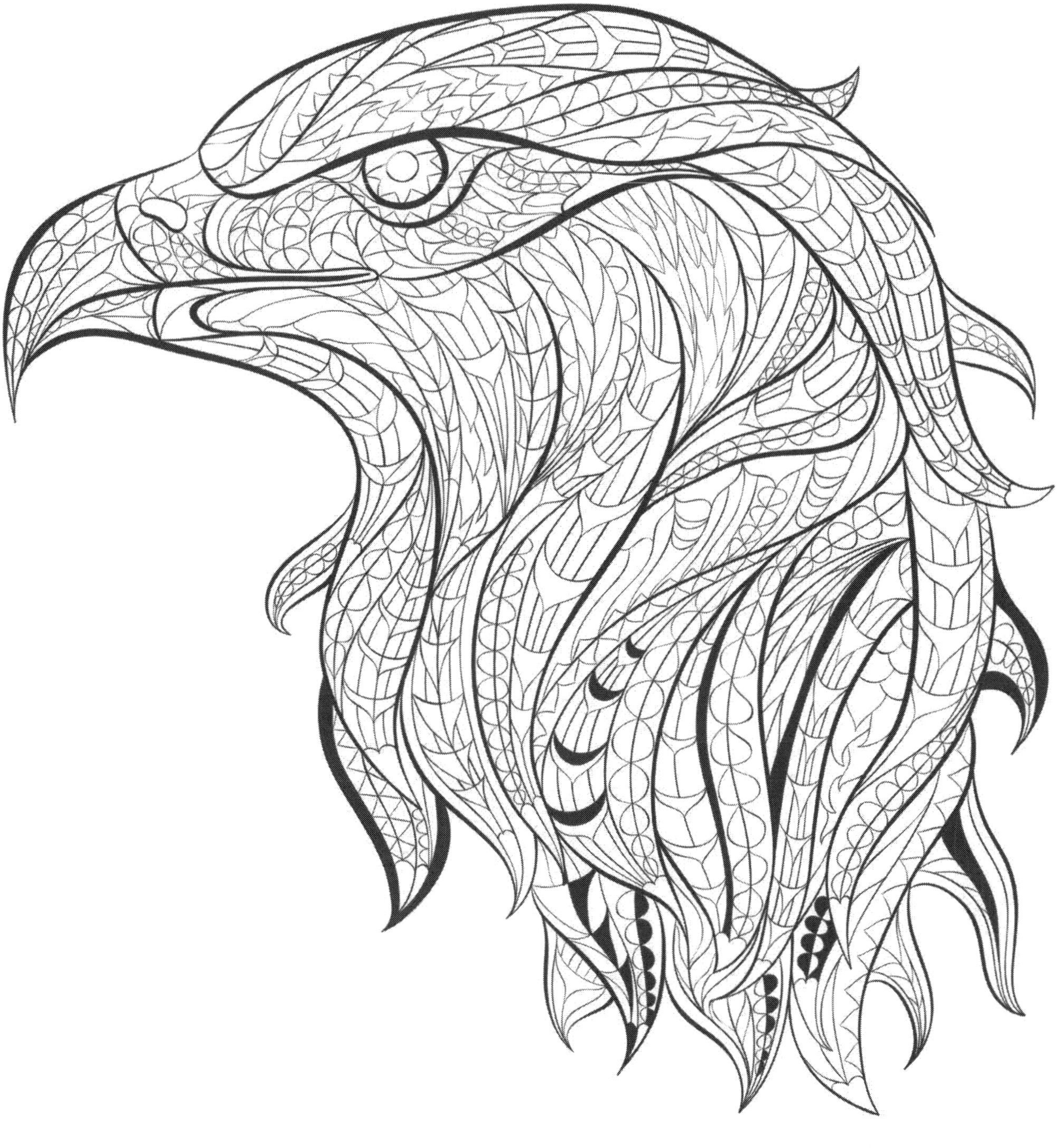

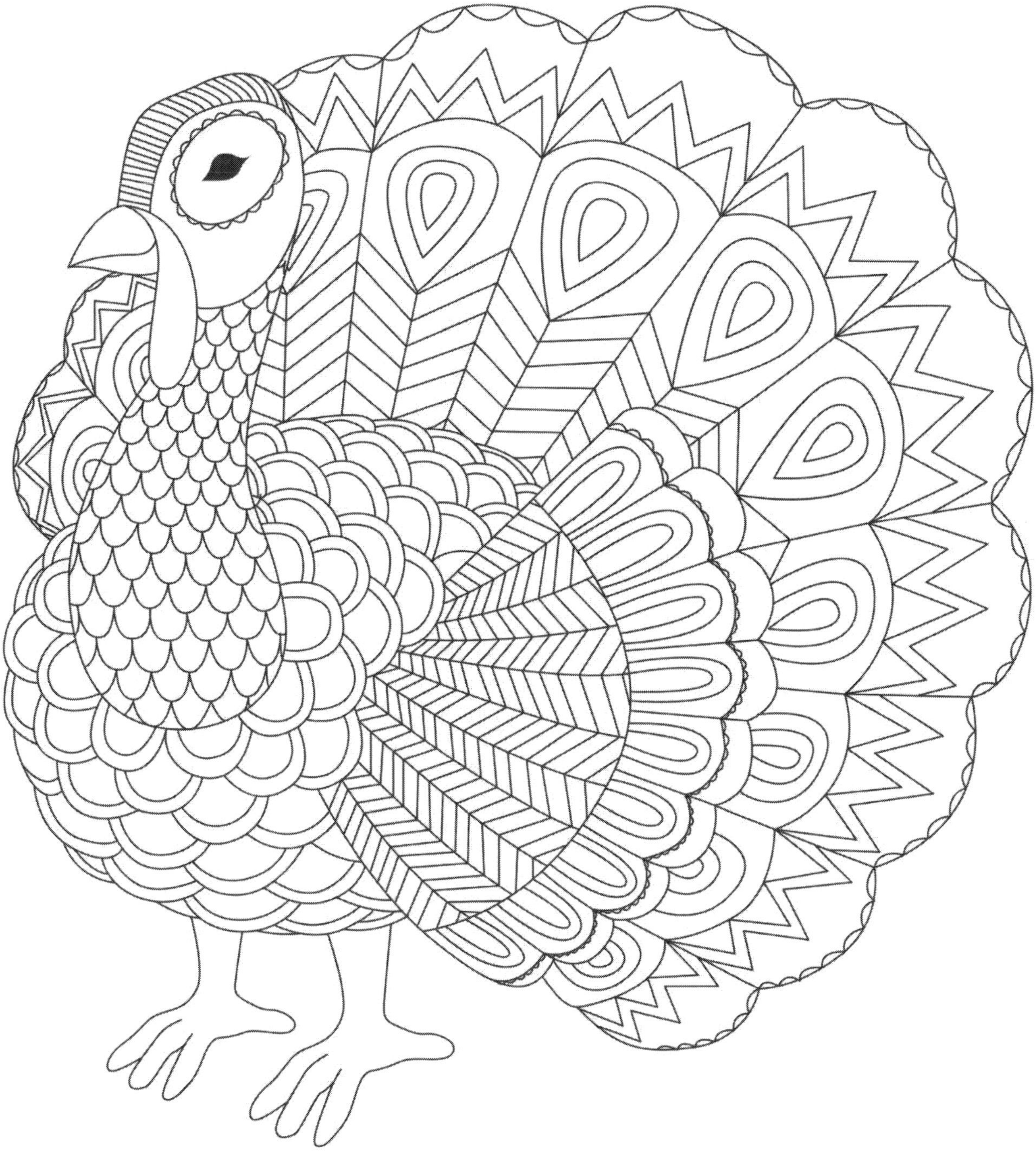

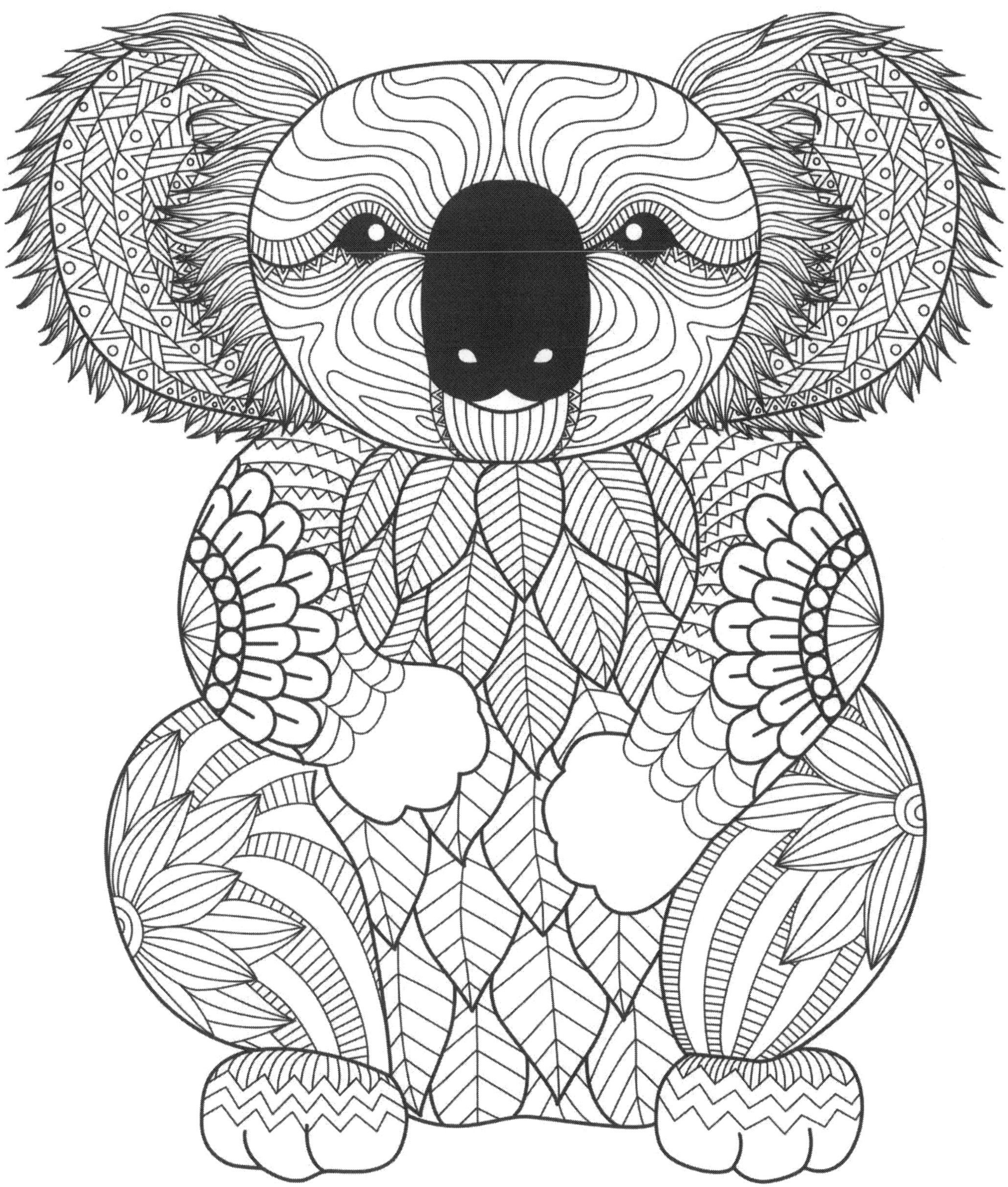

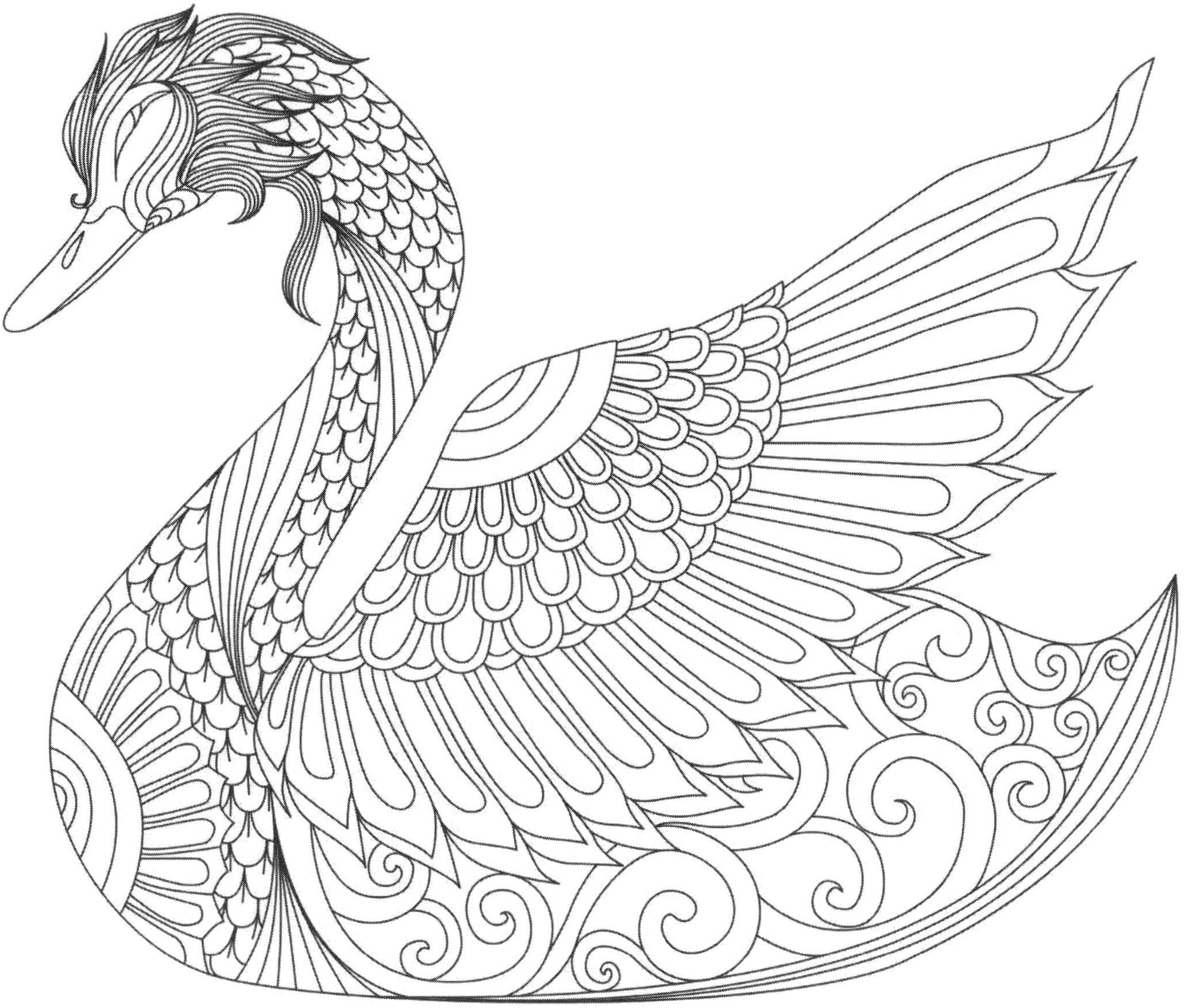

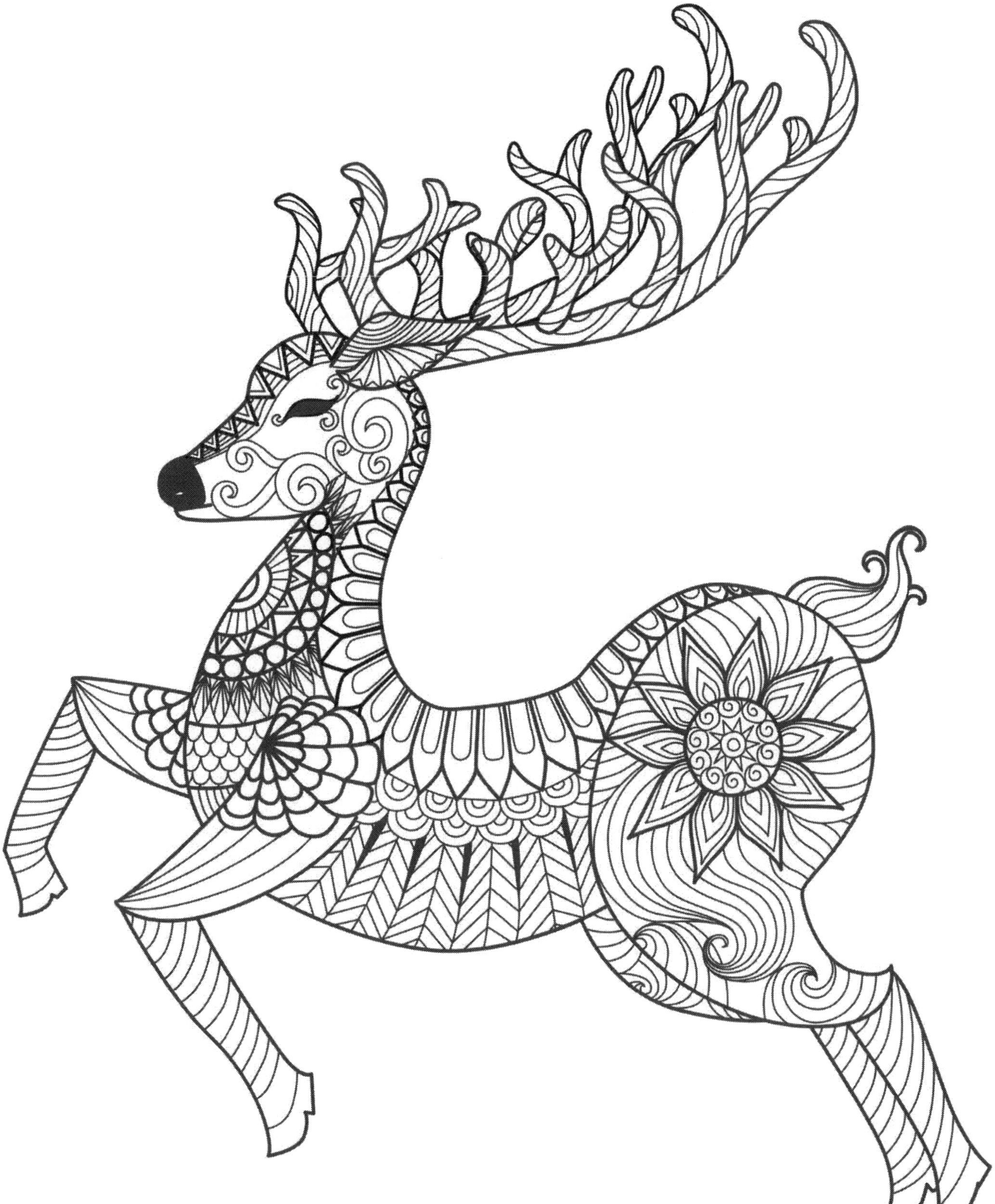

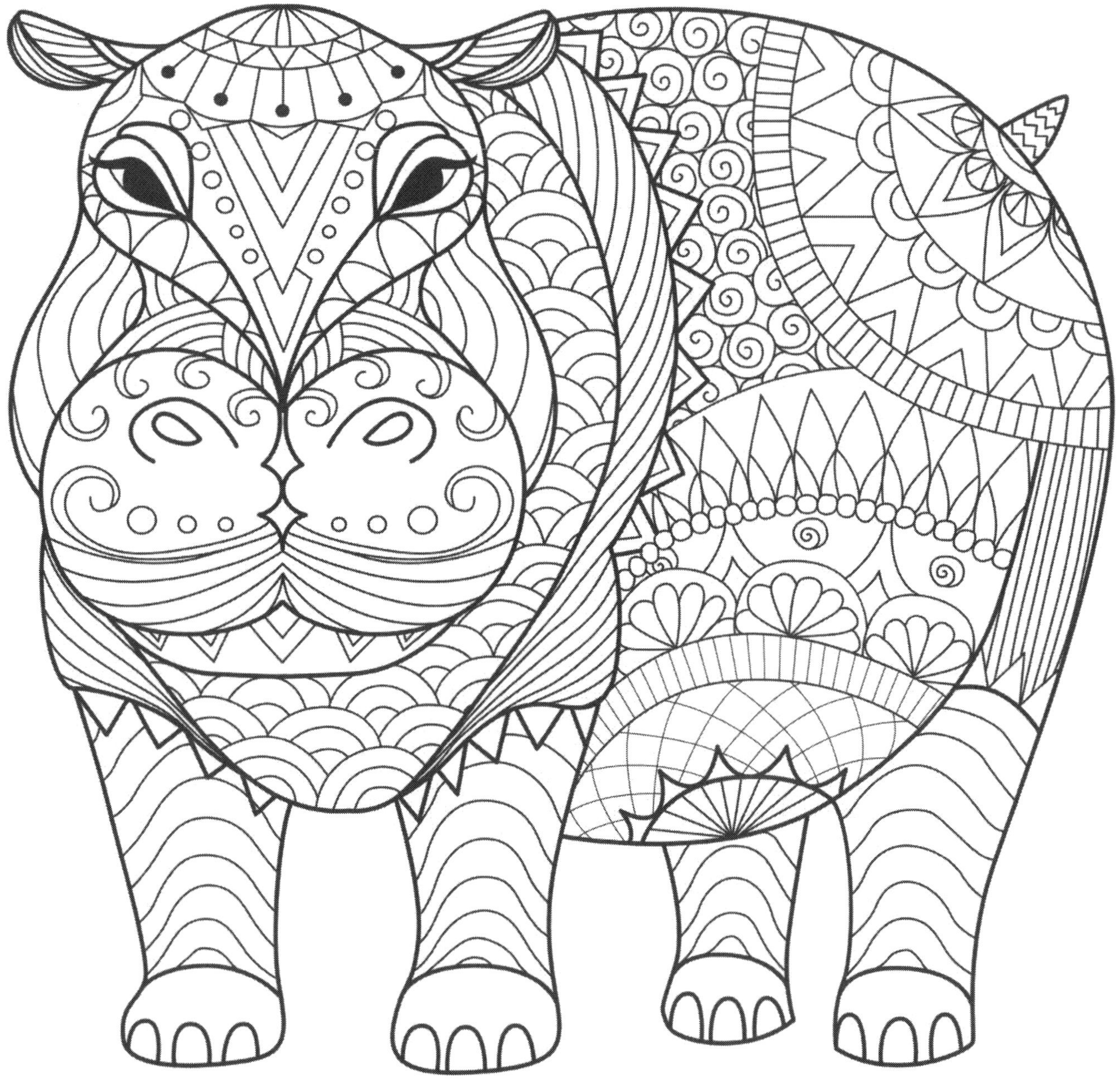

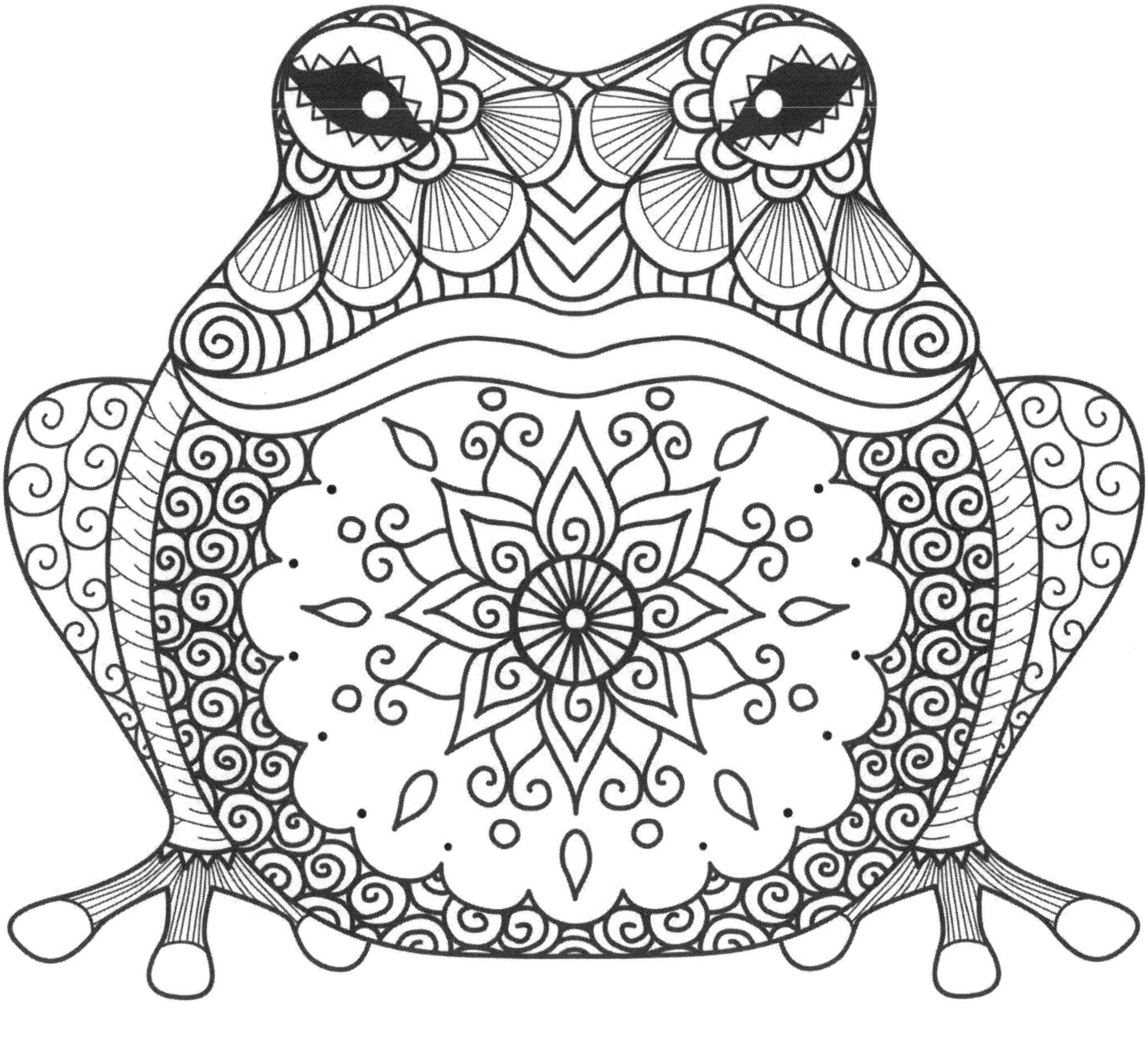

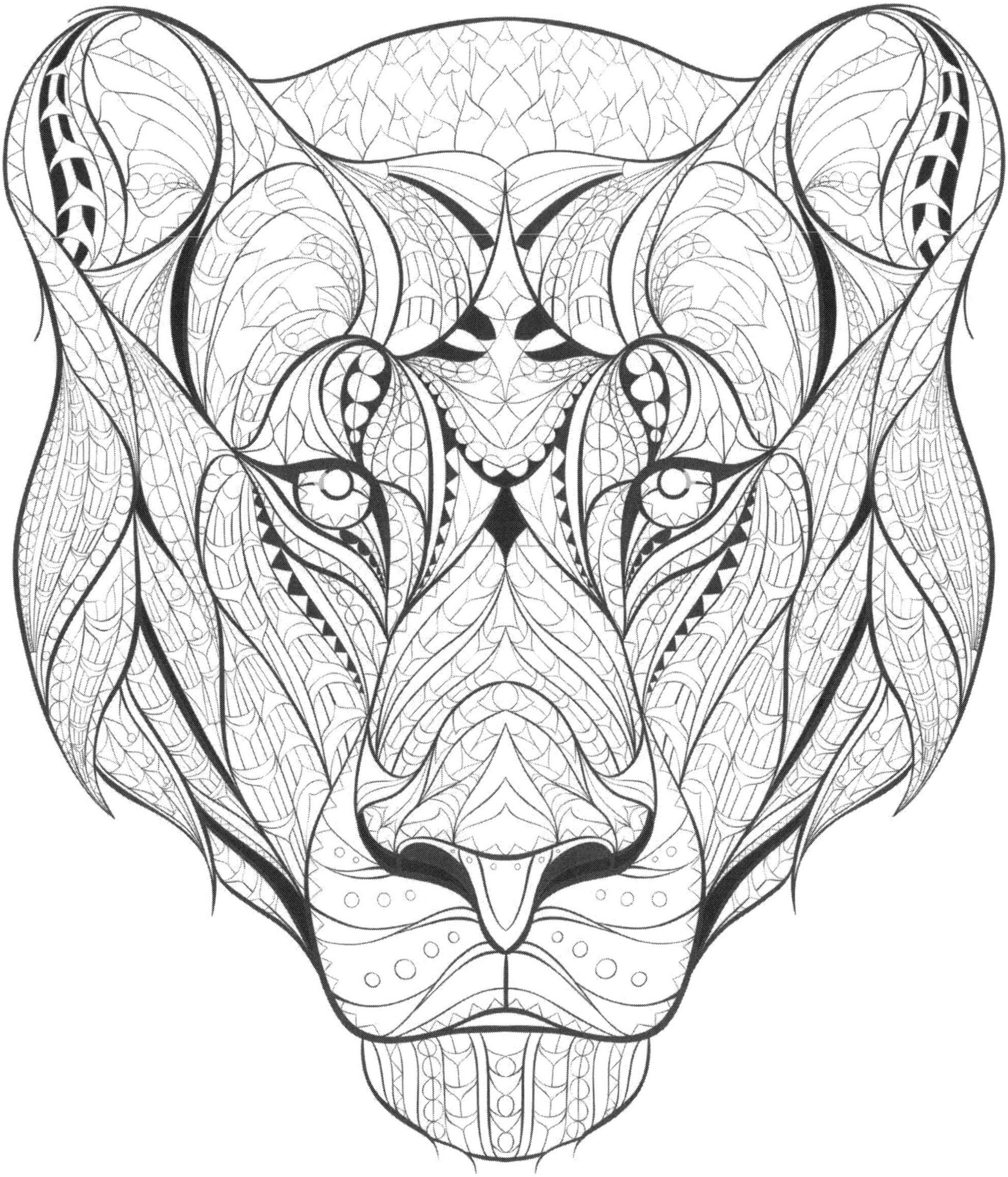

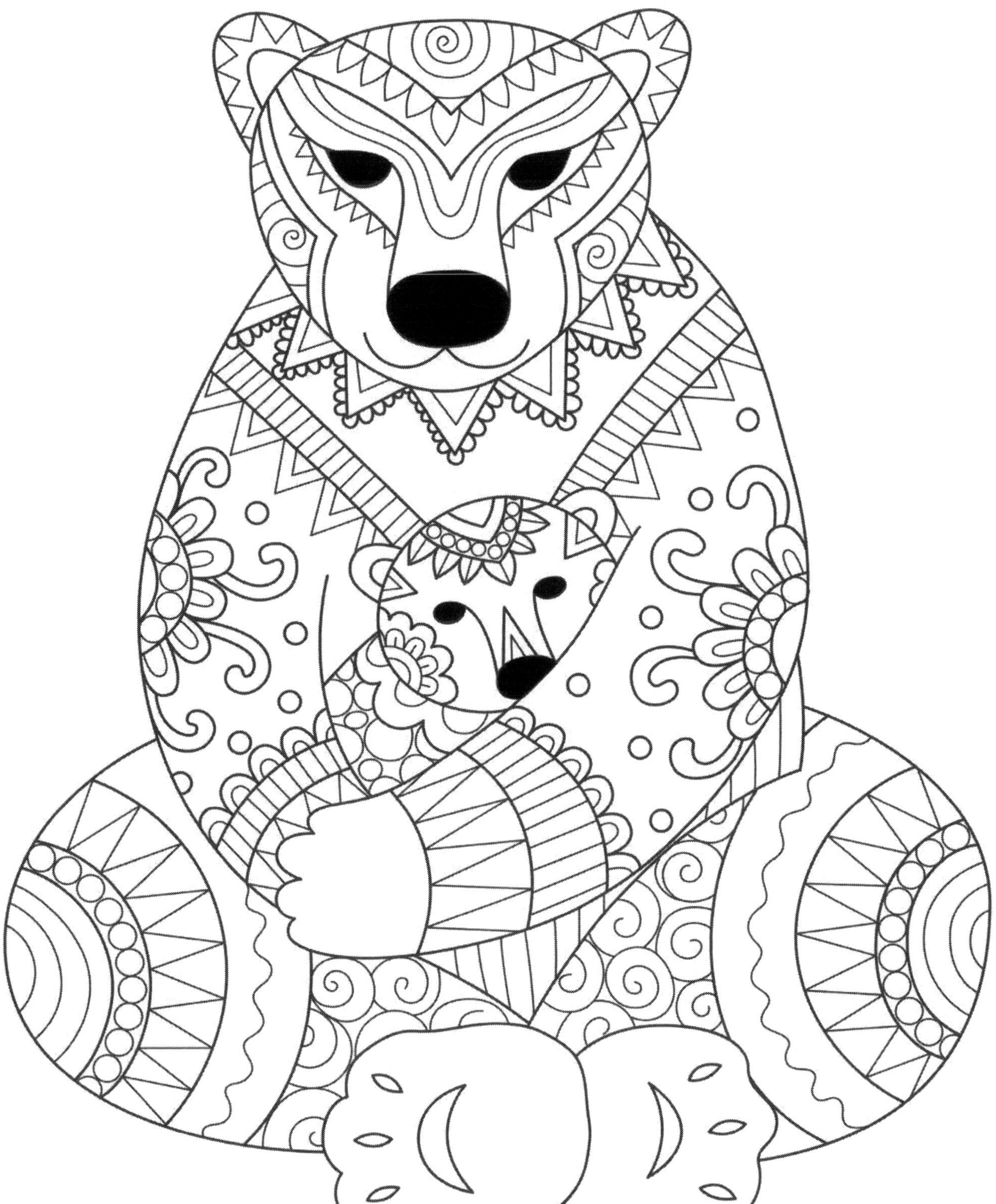

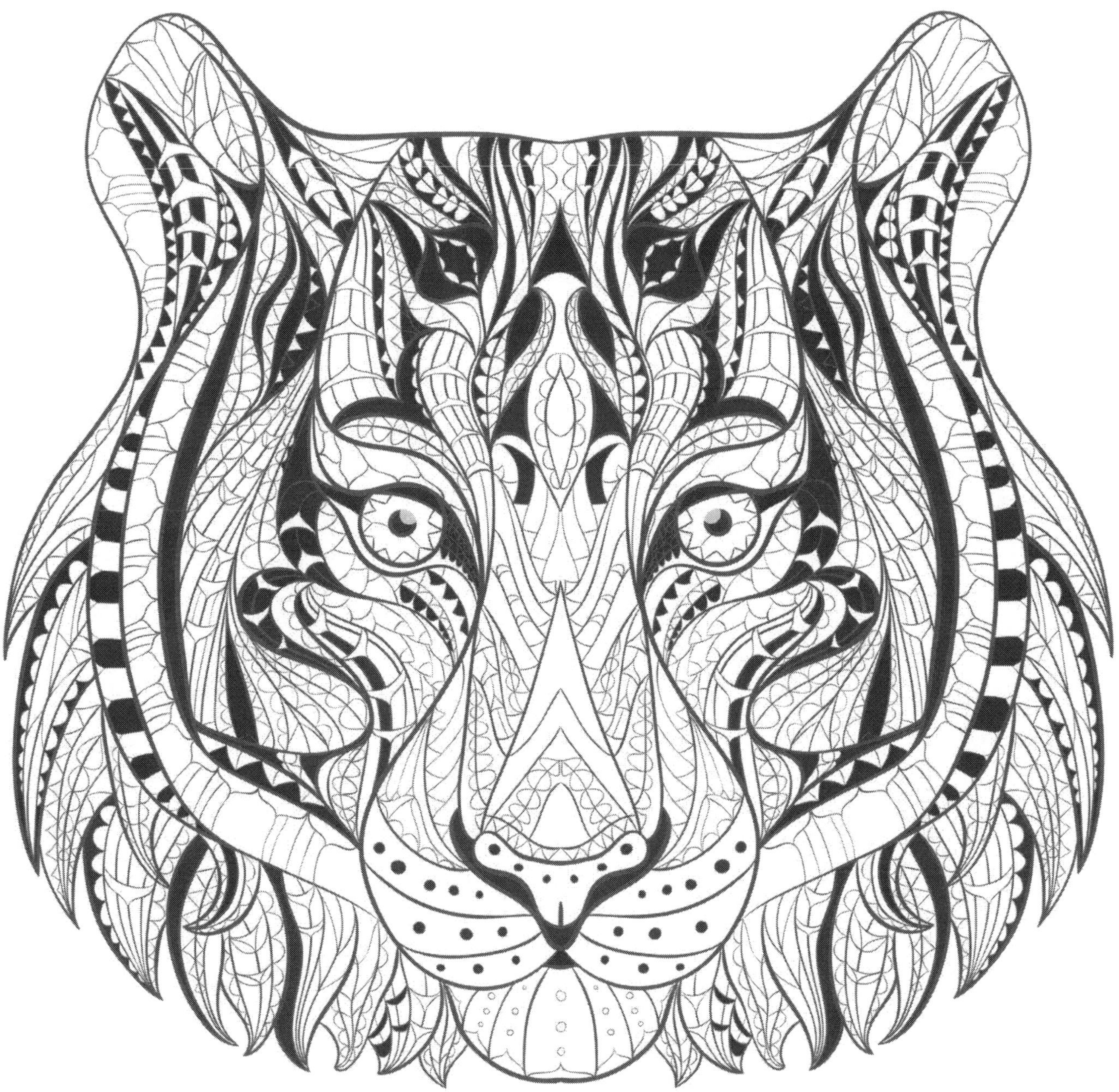

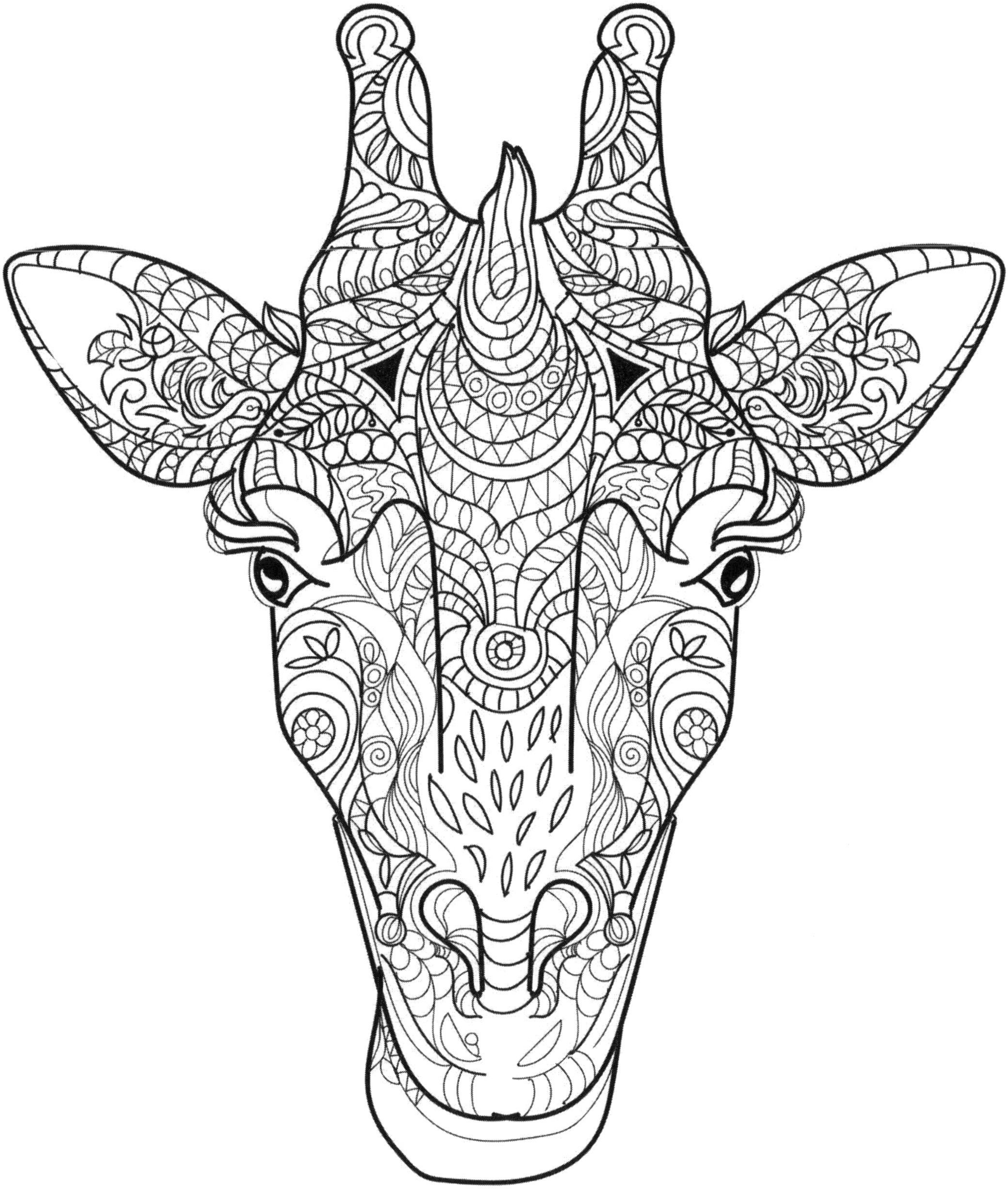

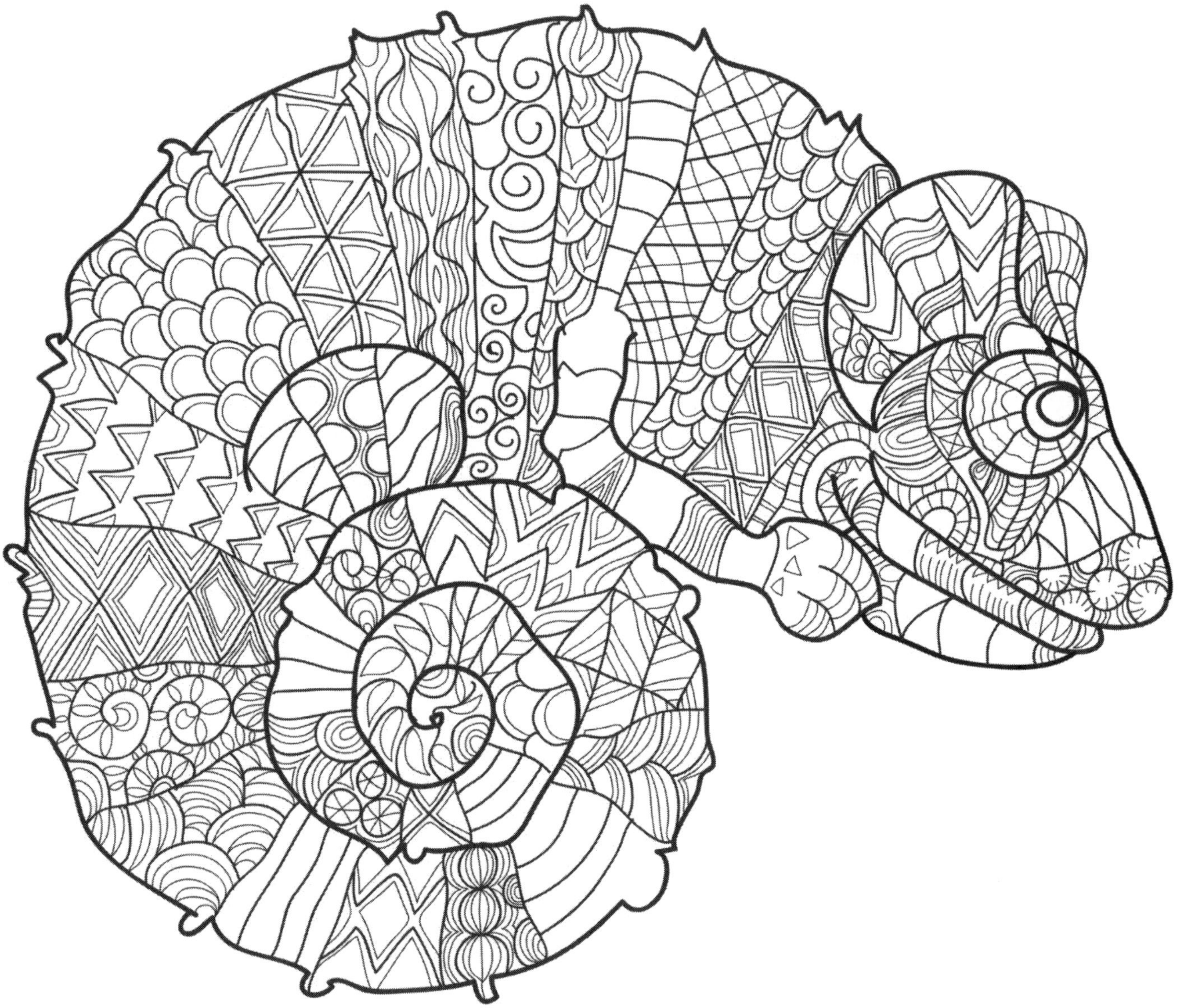

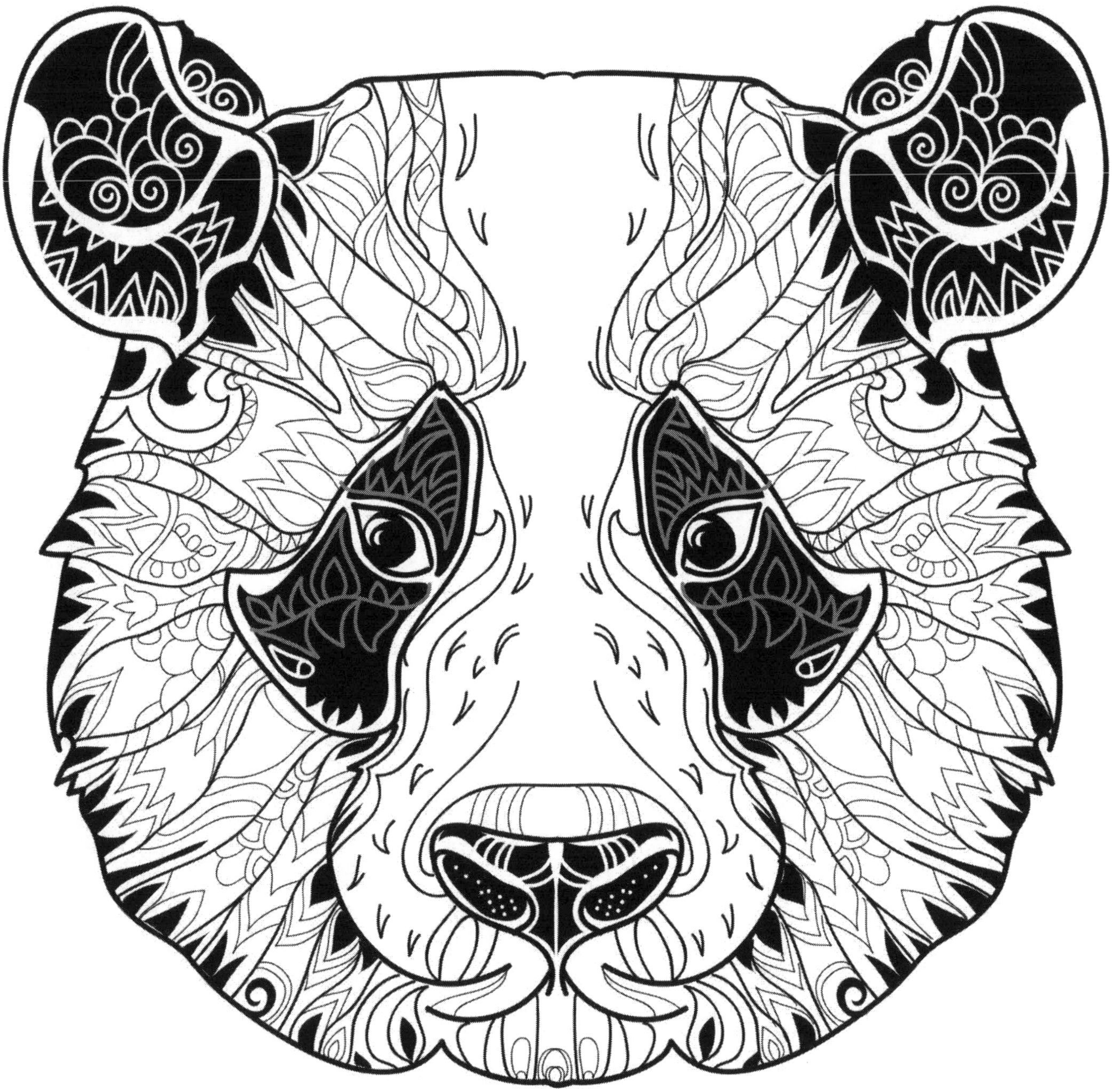

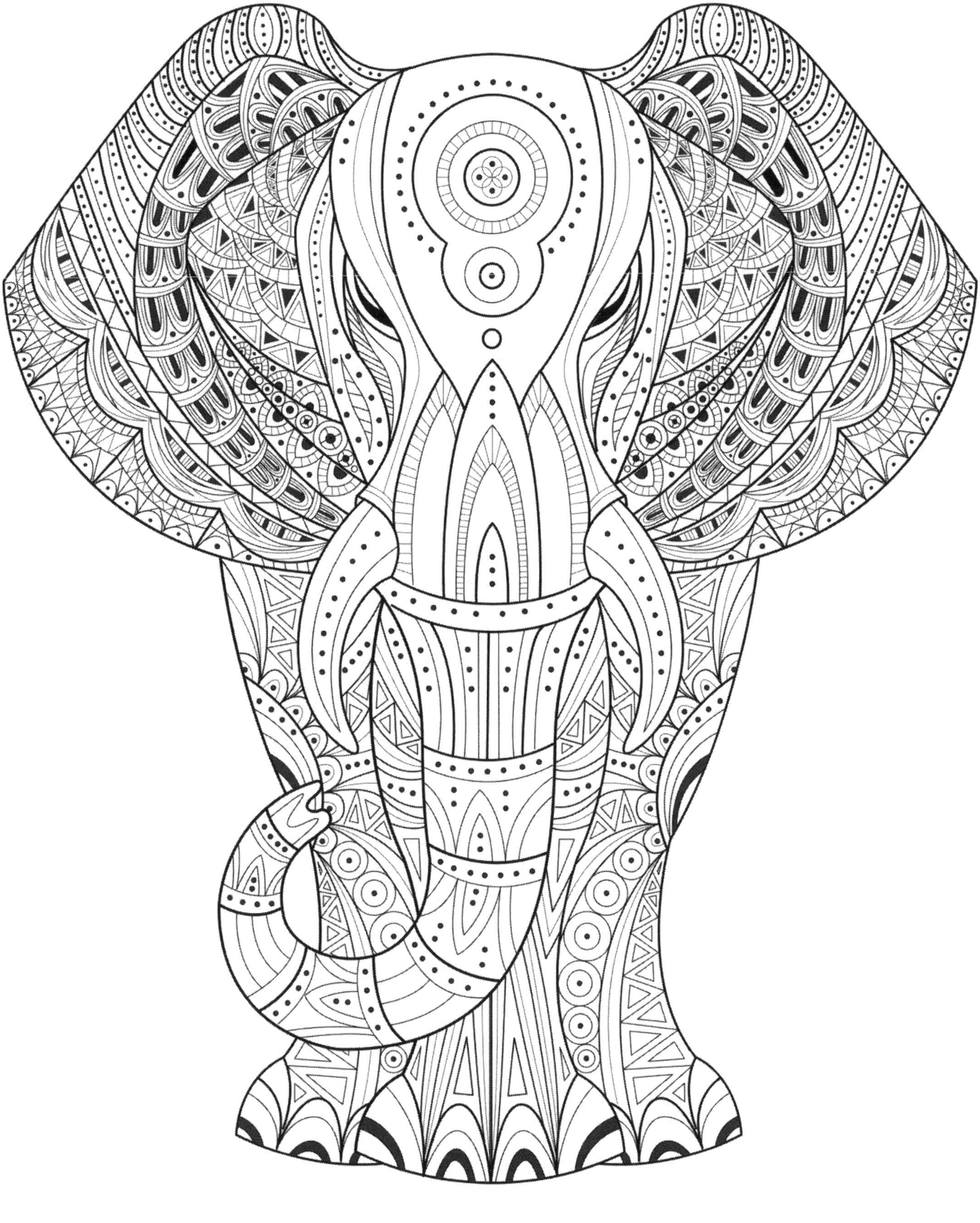

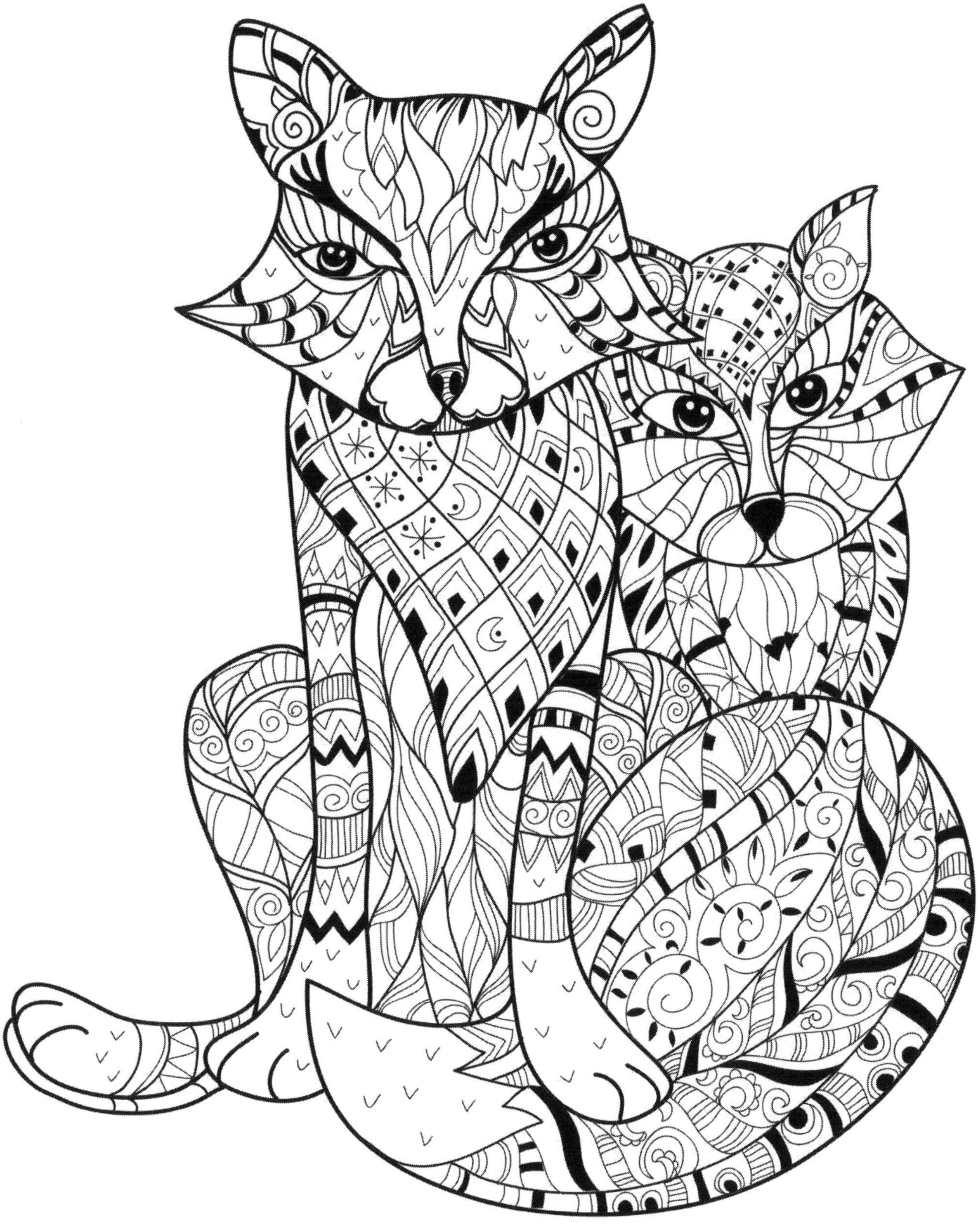

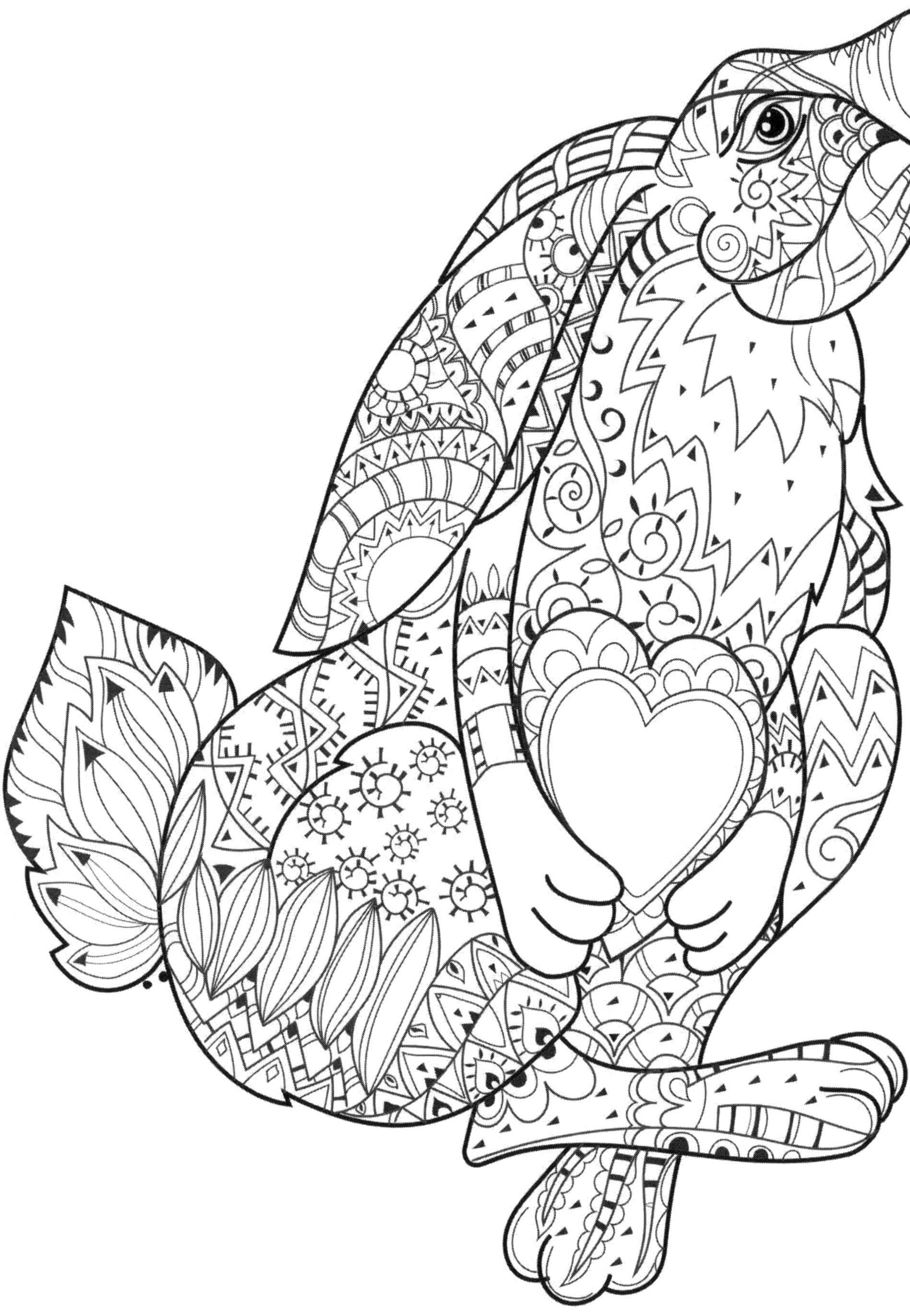

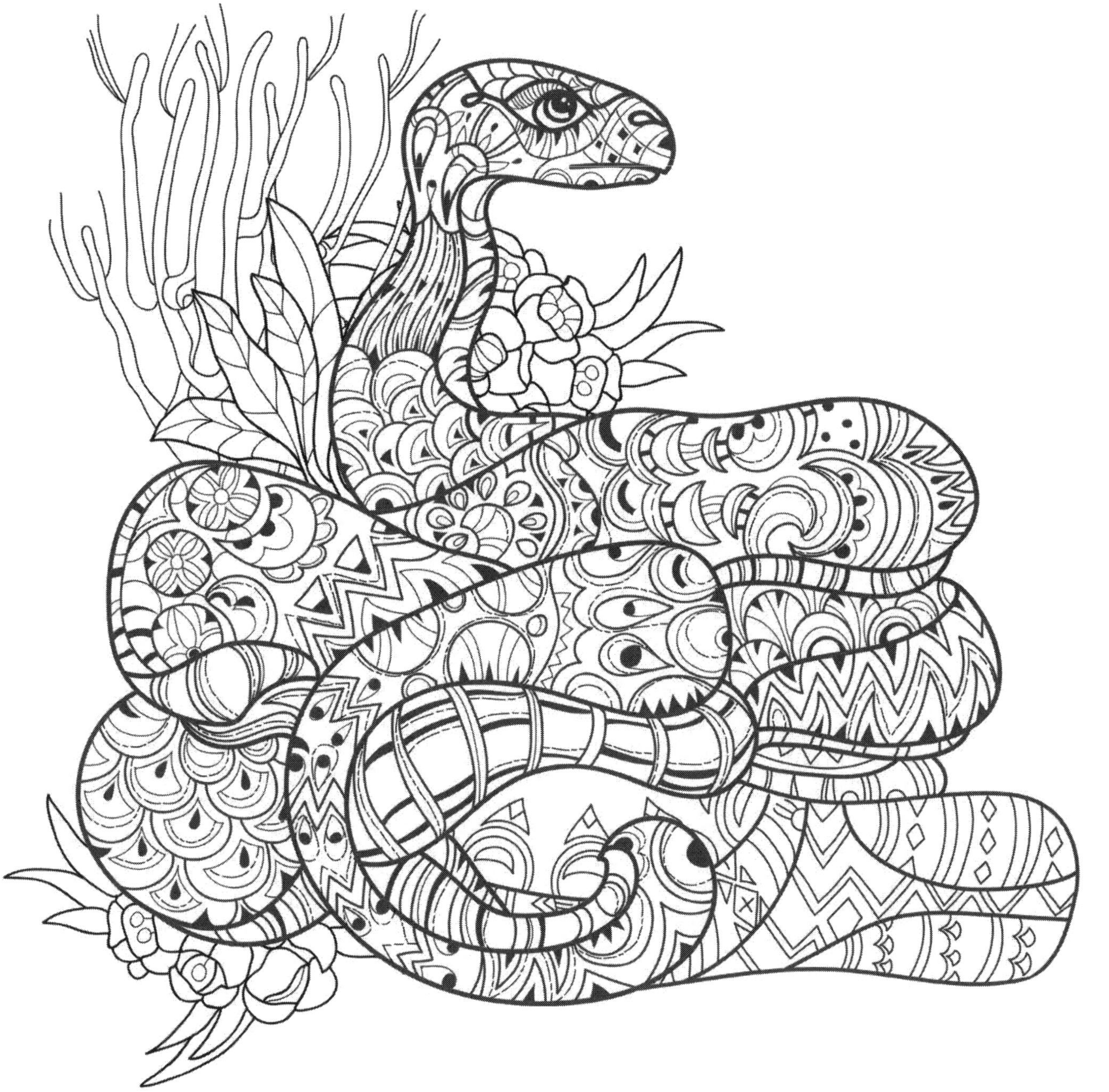

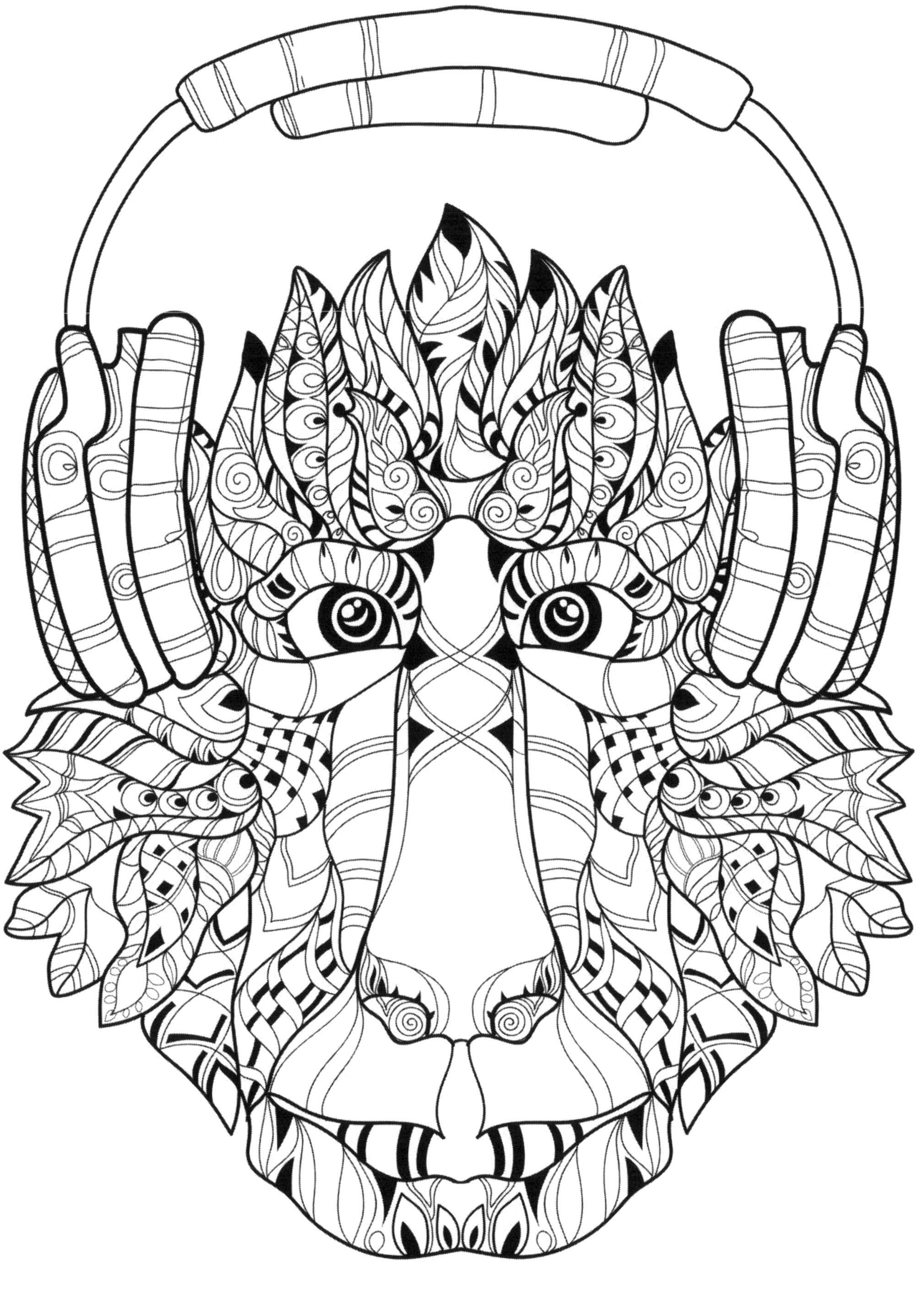

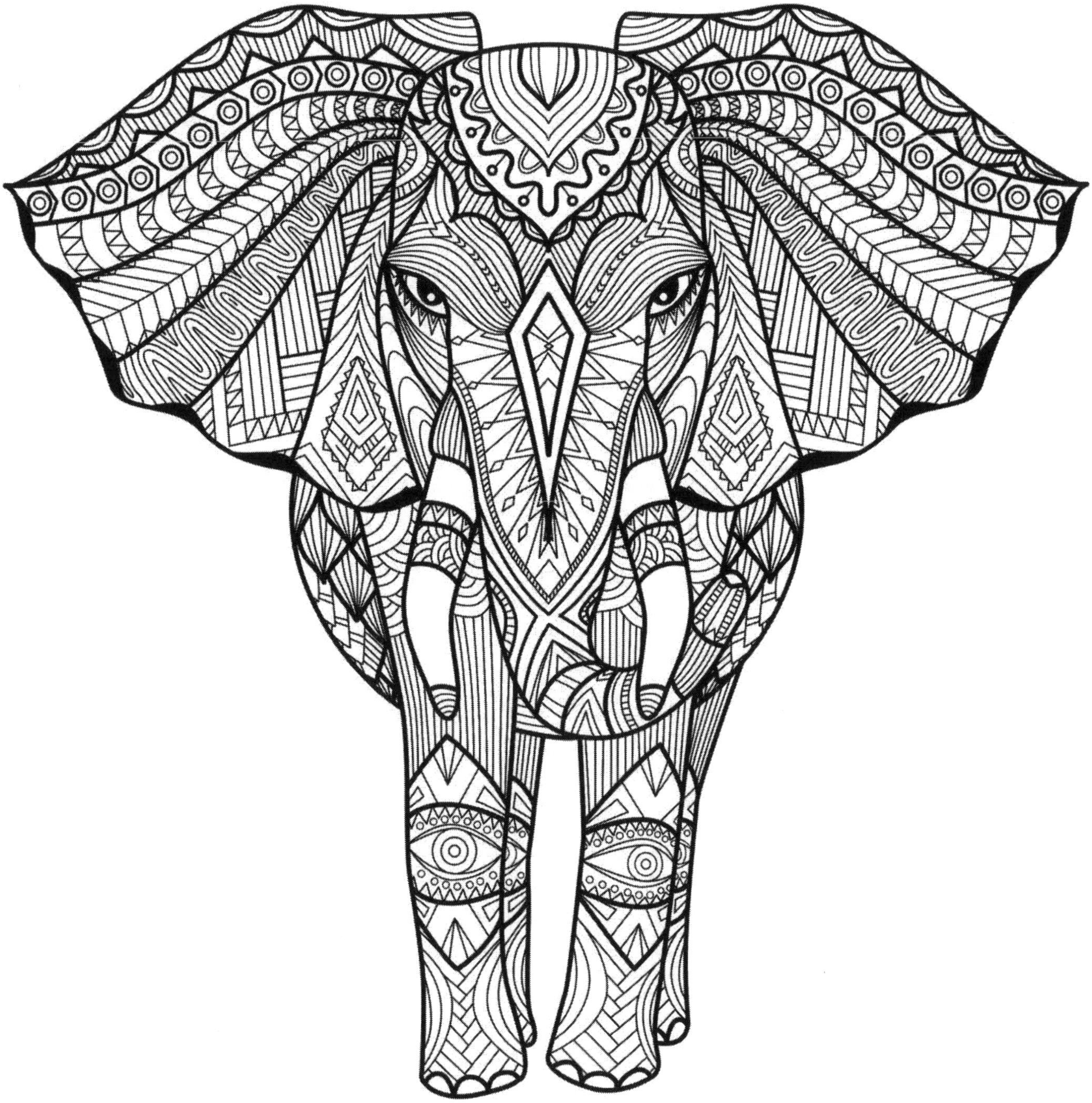

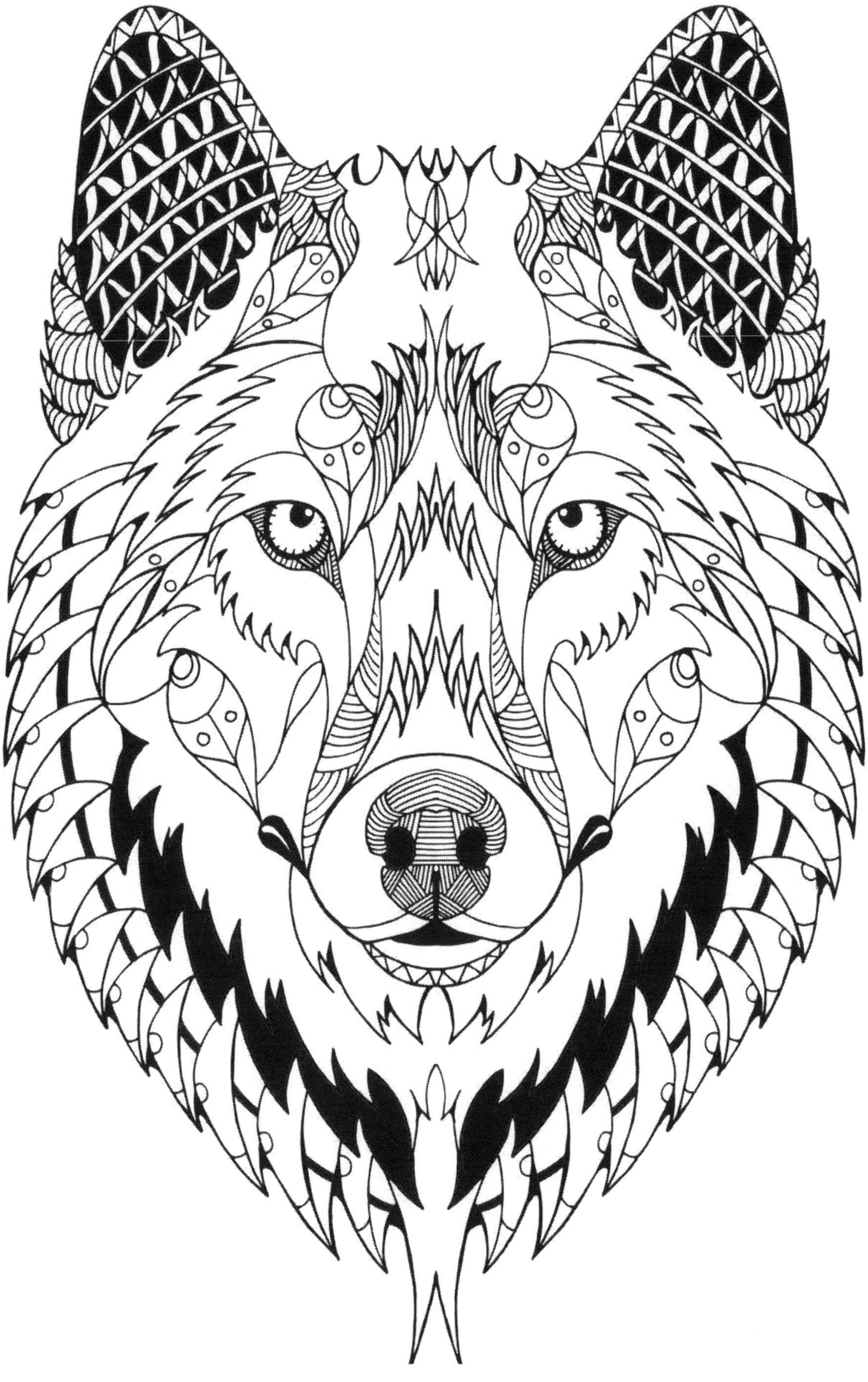

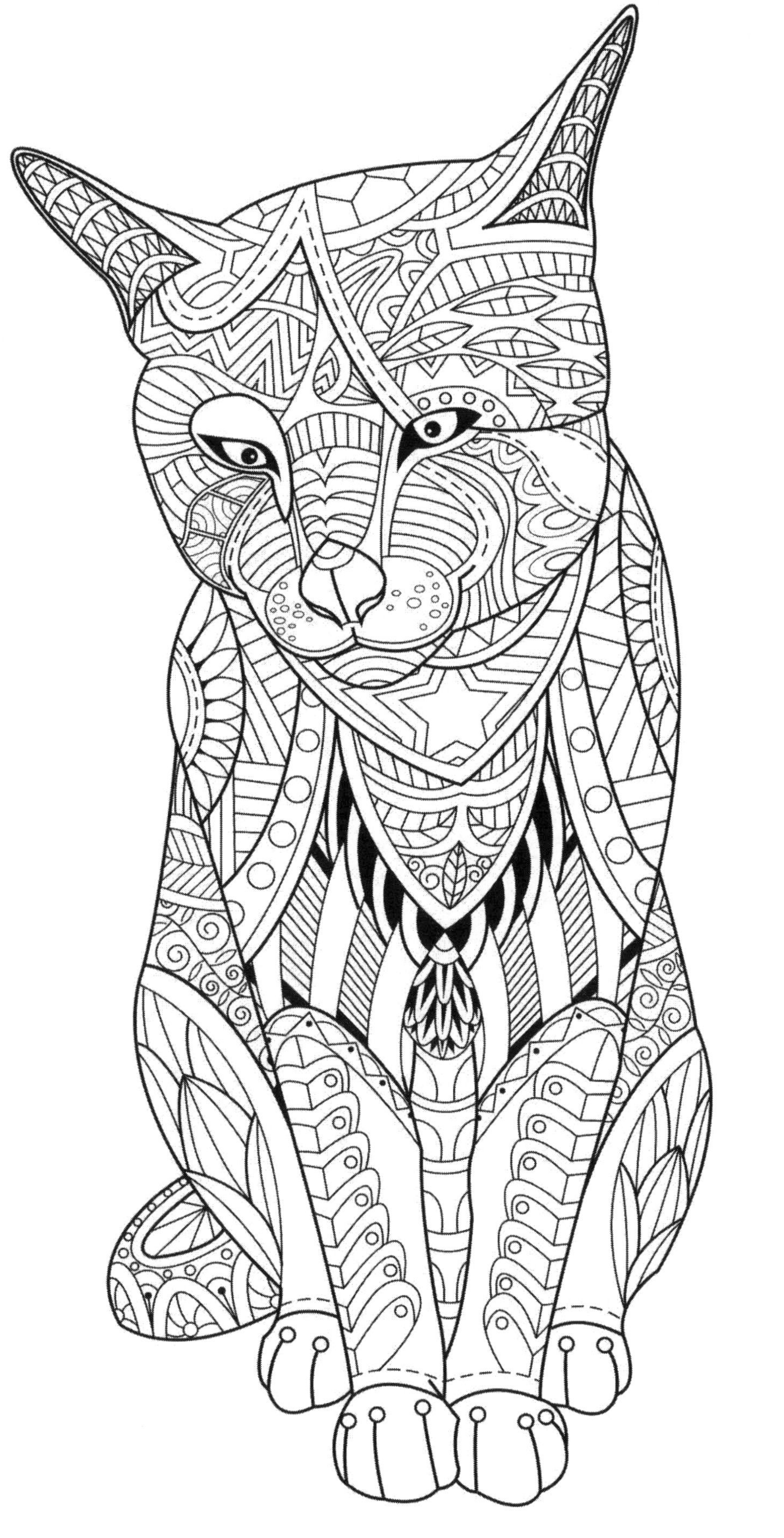

10671006R00040

Made in the USA
San Bernardino, CA
02 December 2018